FOOD LOVERS' LONDON

by

Jenny Linford

Photography by Chris Windsor

Food Lovers' London

Written by Jenny Linford
Cover photograph
by Chris Windsor
Photography by Chris Windsor
Edited by Ally Ireson
Design by Metro Publications

Published in 1999 by
Metro Publications
PO Box 6336
London
N1 6PY
www.metropublications.com

Printed in Great Britain by
The Burlington Press
Foxton
Cambridge
CB2 6SW

British Library Cataloguing in Publication Data.
A catalogue record for this book is available from the British Library.
ISBN 1 902910 03 6

for Mummy, Daddy, Chris and Harry Greenwald

ACKNOWLEDGMENTS

First of all, my thanks to Andrew and Susi at Metro for their enthusiasm, interest and support for the book, Rosie Kindersley for suggesting Metro, and Chris for his time and energy – which has produced some great photographs. Many people spared time to talk to me and my grateful thanks go to the following: everyone I talked to at the BBC World Service; and especially Nina Dekhan, Jon Cannon, Antonio Carluccio, Anna del Conte, Alan Dein, Sarah Edington, Clare Ferguson, Anna Giacon, Pat Howard, Shehzad Husain, the Jewish Chronicle, Sav Kyriacou, Sri Own, Laki Pattelis, Mary Pininska, Claudia Roden, Evelyn Rose, Margaret Shaida, *Siyu* magazine, Yan-Kit So, Marlena Spieler, Jan and Dinah Wieliczko of the Centaur Gallery, John Whiting and, finally, the shopkeepers themselves who patiently answered my many questions and from whom I learned so much.

These are approximate, average prices, per head, for a meal without wine

£	£5-£10
£ £	£10-£15
£ £ £	£15-£25
£ £ £ £	£25-£40
£ £ £ £ £	£40-£60

CONTENTS

J enny Linford lived in Ghana, Trinidad, Singapore and Italy before settling in London, where she now works as a freelance food writer. She has had articles and recipes published in *The Guardian*, *Taste*, *The Times*, *The Illustrated London News* and on Teletext. Her books include *Writing About Food* (A & C Black) and *Tastes of the Orient* (Tesco). An inveterate food shopper, Jenny also founded the highly successful 'Gastro-Soho Tours', which have been running since 1994 (see page 153 for further details).

INTRODUCTION

When I was a child my family moved to Florence and English food took on an especial importance. Visitors were entreated to bring packets of 'ordinary' tea, cheese and onion crisps and Walls' sausages. One small shop near the Duomo, Ye Olde English Store, sold a quaint mixture of English food: tinned asparagus, lemon puffs and Gentleman's Relish. Small jars of Marmite cost a few thousand lire more than they should have but were savoured nevertheless. Now that I am back in London I buy fresh pasta, basil and parmesan and try to recreate the sunny tastes of Tuscany.

This book started out of personal nostalgia but turned into an enjoyable and fascinating journey of discovery. London, where I have lived for so many years, suddenly revealed glimpses into new and varied worlds: the aesthetic delight of a Japanese fish counter, a delicious honey doughnut in a Turkish patisserie, the hustle and bustle of Brixton Market, bagels in a busy Golders Green bakery, being offered a free soft drink in Southall to commemorate a Sikh martyr who had preached tolerance to all. Encounters have been, on the whole, enjoyable (although one Iranian shopowner accused me, only half-jokingly, of being a tax inspector!). Waiting in a Polish bakery while three old ladies bought their rye bread and sausages chatting away in Polish, I gathered, from their sideways glances at me standing notebook in hand, that they were wondering what I was doing there. As one opened her purse to pay the baker, she suddenly broke into English: "Daylight robbery!" she exclaimed, and shot a wicked, amused glance in my direction.

We are so much creatures of habit that new things are avoided almost automatically and this is certainly true with food. One of the great pleasures for me in writing this book has been the discovery of new ingredients and dishes. I had, for example, walked down Drummond Street many times to buy some barfi from the Ambala Sweet Centre but had never stopped to look at the unusual vegetables and fruits on sale. Now I know a little more about them and have tried and enjoyed many. The Japanese say that for every new food tried and truly enjoyed one lives for seventy more days.

In Britain attitudes towards food have changed enormously and more and more specialist ingredients are appearing on supermarket shelves. Supermarkets, however, cannot offer everything or keep it in the best conditions, especially 'exotic' fruit and vegetables. Tired-looking rambutans or rock-hard mangoes in a supermarket compare badly with the excellent quality fruit on offer in Gerrard Street, Asian greengrocer's or West Indian markets. Food is an important part of culture and a primary means of identification. It is a pleasure to shop at places where staff really know what they are selling, from an Italian deli assistant carefully slicing Parma ham to a fishmonger explaining how to cook an unusual fish.

The tragic thing I have witnessed while writing and updating this book is that so many of the smaller shops are being forced to close, with those in central London especially hard hit by steeply rising rents. Small shops are having to open longer to compete with the round-the-clock opening hours offered by supermarkets. As shops like these, run by people who loved and took pride in what they did disappear, we all become impoverished.

1

GENERAL FOODSHOPS

T he shops I have included in this section range from small family businesses passed down from generation to generation, to the vast, impressive food halls which are a characteristic feature of London food shopping.

& Clarke's

BAKER'S

See also under French London.

CENTRAL

Baker & Spice

46 Walton Street, SW3
020-7-589 4734
Tube: South Kensington or Knightsbridge
Open: Mon-Sat 7am-7pm; Sun 8.30am-2pm
From a small, pretty Knightsbridge shop, complete with vintage ovens, a huge array of sophisticated breads, cakes and patisserie is offered, most famously their sourdough loaves with their distinctive tang.

Flour Power City

238 Hoxton Street, N1
(020-7-729 7414)
Tube: Old Street
Open: Mon-Sat 8am-2pm
Matthew Jones (formerly at Mezzo's bakery) has recently opened this basic bakery where, he says, "the bread comes from oven to counter". Business is already booming, as bread-lovers discover the joys of Matthew's organic City Sour (an open-textured sourdough bread made from a fermented potato starter), organic ciabatta and sourdough focaccia flavoured with rosemary, seasalt and olive oil.

De Gustibus

53 Blandford Street, W1
(020-7-486 6608)
Tube: Baker Street
Open: Mon-Fri 7am-4.30pm
This small café is an outlet for Oxfordshire-based baker Dan Schickentanz, which offers a range of his excellent breads, including the famous Six Day Sour (made with a sourdough starter) and Milwaukee Rye. The lunchtime trade is offered goodies such as tortino, vegetarian pasta dishes and superior sandwiches made with Dan's breads.

6 Suffolk Street, SE1
Tube: London Bridge
A new London branch offering treats baked on the premises, ranging from focaccia to Dan's famous rye breads.

Konditor & Cook

27 Cornwall Road, SE1
(020-7-261 0456)
Tube: Waterloo
Open: Mon-Fri 7.30am-6.30pm;
Sat 8.30am-2pm
Gerhard Jenne's bakery is noted for its creative cakes and pastries, from wildly colourful iced gingerbread skeletons at Halloween to imaginatively personalised birthday cakes (much in demand with celebrity clients). One reason for Gerhard's success is that he firmly believes everything should taste as good as it looks.
Also at *10 Stoney Street, SE1*
(020-7-407 5100)

WEST

& Clarke's

122 Kensington Church Street, W8
(020-7-229 2190)
Tube: High Street Kensington
Open: Mon-Fri 8am-8pm; Sat 9am-4pm
An elegantly rustic shop next door to Sally Clarke's restaurant, this sells her famous breads, such as rosemary, raisin and sea-salt; and a selection of excellent goods such as chocolate cake, tarts, and sweet and savoury biscuits. Additional stock includes Neal's Yard Dairy and Innes cheeses, delectable homemade chocolate truffles, homemade chutneys, crisps, fresh Gospel Green Cider, and a select choice of seasonal British produce.
There is a small café section at the back of the shop at which to sit and sample the shop's baked delicacies.

BUTCHER'S

Even the most basic high-street butcher's is a fast-vanishing breed, while a really decent one is extremely hard to find. One encouraging thing to emerge from the BSE crisis is that those butchers who put the emphasis on providing quality, plant-fed, free-range or organic meat have seen sales improve, as customers realise the value of buying meat from a trustworthy source.

CENTRAL LONDON

Allen & Co.
117 Mount Street, W1
(020-7-499 5831/629 1291)
Tube: Bond Street
Open: Mon-Fri 3.30am-4pm;
Sat 3.30am-12.30pm
With its beautiful tiles and huge wooden chopping blocks, this venerable butchers is a Mayfair institution with customers ranging from film stars to famous restaurants. Allen & Co. is noted for the quality and range of its game and also for its Scotch beef.

Biggles
66 Marylebone Lane, W1
(020-7-224 5937)
Tube: Bond Street
Open: Mon-Sat 9.30am-4.30pm;
Tue-Fri 9.30am-6pm
Tucked away down a charming street, Biggles is a sausage specialist selling made-on-the-premises, high-meat sausages in a huge range of varieties, from Toulouse to Greek.

Portwine
6 Earlham Street, WC2
(020-7-836 2353)
Tube: Leicester Square
Open: Mon & Sat 7.30am-2pm;
Tue-Thur 7.30am-5pm; Fri 7.30am-5.30pm
Run with enthusiasm by Graham Portwine, who can proudly say that there's been a Portwine butcher's shop in the Seven Dials area since 1790, this small shop specialises in traditional quality meat. Stock includes meat from rare breeds, MacSween haggis, game, geese and excellent dry-cured bacon.

Simply Sausages
Harts Corner, 341 Central Markets
Farringdon Street, EC1
(020-7-329 3227)
Tube: Farringdon
Open: Mon-Fri 8am-6pm; Sat 9.30am-2pm
Appropriately next to Smithfield meat market, this corner shop sells over 40 different seasonal sausages at any time of the year. In addition to truly meaty sausages – such as venison or pork – seafood and vegetarian sausages are also stocked.
Also at: *93 Berwick Street, W1*
(020-7-287 3482)

EAST

Leadenhall Market,
off Leadenhall Street, EC3
Tube: Aldgate
Open: Mon-Fri 8am-4pm
Inside this picturesque Victorian arcade in the shadow of the Lloyds Building, is a selection of upmarket butcher's and fishmonger's, whose quality stock reflects the world of huntin', fishin' and shootin'. Venerable fishmonger's include Ashdown, at 23 Leadenhall Market (020-7-626 3871), which specialises in hand-sliced smoked salmon and live lobsters and oysters; and H. S. Linwood, 6-7 Grand Avenue (020-7-929 0554). Butcher's R. S. Ashby, at 8 & 9 Leadenhall Market (020-7-626 3871), is known for Scotch beef; while Butcher & Edmonds, at 1, 2 & 3 Grand Avenue (020-7-626 5816), specialises in game.

Portwine

NORTH

Frank Godfrey Ltd
7 Highbury Park, N5
(020-7-226 2425)
Tube: Arsenal
Open: Mon-Fri 8am-6pm; Sat 9am-5pm
This down-to-earth family butcher's – now run by fourth generation brothers Chris and Jeremy Godfrey – has a loyal and devoted following who know good meat when they see it. All the meat sold here is free-range and very good quality, from the English corn-fed chickens to the plant-fed pork and Orkney Island beef. The brothers work closely with their suppliers to ensure high feed and welfare standards, and the results are reflected in the meat that they sell.

Graham's
134 East End Road, N2
(020-8-883 6187)
Tube: East Finchley or Finchley Central
Open: Tue-Fri 7.30am-5.30pm;
Sat 7.30am-4pm; Sun 9am-1pm
Among the specialities on offer are Aberdeen Angus beef, free-range meat and organic poultry. Food writer John Whiting recommends the free-range pork.

Highland Organics
14 Bittacy Hill, NW7
(020-8-346 1055)
Tube: Mill Hill
Open: Mon-Sat 8am-6pm
As the name suggests, organic meats are on offer here, from Welsh black cattle beef steaks to huge plump homemade sausages. Customers can also stock up on basic organic groceries, from fresh bread to baked beans.

Midhurst
2 Midhurst Parade, N10
(020-8-883 5303)
Tube: East Finchley, then the 102 bus
Open: Mon-Thur 8am-6pm;
Fri 7am-6pm; Sat 7am-5pm

Tucked away in a little parade of shops between Muswell Hill and East Finchley, this small shop offers decent meat (some organic) and a picturesque range of fresh fruit and veg outside.

SOUTH-EAST LONDON

P. & J. Baker
147 Evelina Road, SE15
(020-7-732 2820)
BR: Nunhead
Open: Tues-Sat 6am-5.30pm
A cheerful family-run butchers where popular items include excellent homemade pork bangers (made to a 100 year old recipe), well-hung beef and free-range chickens.

Kennedy's
85 Rye Lane, SE15
(020-7-639 1288)
BR: Peckham Rye
Open: Mon-Fri 8am-5pm; Sat 8am-4pm
Simple, down-to-earth, old-fashioned pork sausages are what Kennedy's are known for – their string of shops extends across South-East London.

SOUTH-WEST

Arkwrights
20 Barnes High Street, SW13
(020-8-878 1520)
BR: Barnes or Barnes Bridge
Open: Mon-Fri 9am-6pm; Sat 9am-5.30pm
This smart sausage shop has an upmarket and imaginative range of homemade bangers on offer: from bestselling Garlic Toulouse to novelties such as Szechuan Duck (flavoured with aromatic star anise) or vegetarian Carrot, Orange and Lentil.

A. Dove & Son
71 Northcote Road, SW11
(020-7-223 5191)
BR: Clapham Junction
Open: Mon 8am-1pm; Tue-Sat 8am-6pm

This characterful butcher's shop, run with passion by Bob Dove, has a loyal clientele. Particular highlights include the well-hung beef, Linda Dove's frozen meat pies and excellent bronze turkeys.

Lindy's of Richmond
1 Duke Street, TW9
(020-8-940 1220)
Tube: Richmond
Open: Mon-Fri 9.30am-4pm; Sat 9am-5pm
This small, tucked-away shop offers an excellent choice of own-made sausages. Bestsellers include Thai Pork & Chilli and Italiano (with fennel, garlic and herbs). Lunchtime customers can sample the wares by buying a take-away sausage sandwich.

M. Moen & Sons
24 The Pavement, SW4
(020-7-622 1624)
Tube: Clapham Common
Open: Mon-Fri 8am-6.30pm; Sat 7.30am-5pm
This well-established butcher's offers a distinctly upmarket stock. The meat is good quality, from homemade sausages to a range of in-season game. Additional delights include wild mushrooms and seasonal produce like sea-kale.

Pether
16 Station Parade, TW9
Kew Gardens
(020-8-940 0163)
Tube: Kew Gardens
Open: Mon-Fri 7.30am-6pm; Sat 7.30am-5pm
An appetising smell of spit-roasted chicken wafts out from this old-fashioned butcher's. All the meat here is free-range and the shop does a roaring trade in homemade pies.

WEST

Kingsland Edwardian Butchers
140 Portobello Road, W11
Tube: Notting Hill
Open: Mon-Sat 7.30am-6pm

A bright red frontage marks out this attractive, old-fashioned butcher's shop (as seen in the film *Notting Hill*). There is a good range of meat, from their own dry-cured bacon to Orkney Aberdeen Angus beef. The speciality here, however, is rare breeds meat, from Gloucester Old Spot pork to extremely rare, seaweed-fed North Ronaldsay lamb from Orkney. Staff are both jocular and helpful.

C. Lidgate
110 Holland Park Avenue, W11
(020-7-727 8243)
Tube: Holland Park
Open: Mon-Thur 7.30am-6pm;
Fri 7am-6pm; Sat 7am-5pm
A grand old butcher's established in 1850, which specialises in high-quality, naturally-grown and fed meat and poultry. Run with great expertise and commitment by David Lidgate, the shop's stock includes organic meat from Highgrove (the estate of The Prince of Wales), free-range bronze turkeys and geese. In addition, this family business sells award-winning homemade pies such as steak and kidney, and own-cooked hams.

Macken Bros
44 Turnham Green Terrace, W4
(020-8-994 2646)
Tube: Turnham Green
Open: Mon-Fri 7am-6pm; Sat 7am-5.30pm
A seemingly perpetual queue testifies to this shop's popularity. Staff are helpful and friendly and the meat and poultry excellent.

Richardsons
88 Northfield Avenue, W13
(020-8-567 1064)
Open: Mon-Thur 8am-5.30pm; Fri 8am-6pm;
Sat 8am-4.30pm
A member of the Queen's Guild of Butchers, this down-to-earth, busy butcher's attracts loyal customers, brought back by the quality of the meat on offer, which includes well hung beef and award-winning sausages.

7

CHEESE SHOPS

Neil's Yard Dairy

CENTRAL

Neal's Yard Dairy
17 Shorts Gardens, WC2
(020-7-379 7646)
Tube: Covent Garden
Open: Mon-Sat 9am-7pm; Sun 11am-5pm
A pioneering champion of British farm
cheeses, this small dairy shop has an
impressive range of farmhouse cheeses
including classics such as Appleby's Cheshire,
Keen's Cheddar and Mrs Kirkham's
Lancaster. Other produce includes Mr Haw's
traditional fruit 'cheeses', Clarke's breads and
good quality cream, yogurt and butter. Staff
are both friendly and knowledgeable and
customers are encouraged to taste before
buying – one of the joys of artisanal-made
cheese is that they vary in flavour from batch
to batch.
Also at: *6 Park Street, SE1 (020-7-407 1800)*

Paxton & Whitfield
93 Jermyn Street, SW1
(020-7-930 0259)
Tube: Piccadilly Circus
Open: Mon-Sat 9am-5.30pm
This picturesque, vintage shop (over 200
years old) is a well-known name in cheese-
selling. Staff are helpful and there is a good
range of over 200 classic cheeses from
Stilton to chestnut leaf-wrapped Banon
goat's cheese, plus an assortment of wafers,
biscuits and relishes.

Rippon Cheese Stores
26 Upper Tachbrook Street, SW1
(020-7-931 0628)
Tube: Pimlico or Victoria
Open: Mon-Sat 8am-6.30pm
In this cool, neat shop Karen and Philip
Rippon stock an astonishing range of around
550 European cheeses. Here, one can find
seven different Cheddars, six different bries
and a range of differently aged Crottin.
Stock is clearly priced and labelled and Karen
and Philip are very happy to offer advice.

NORTH

Barstow & Barr
204 Upper Street, N1
(020-7-359 4222)
Tube: Angel
Open: Mon-Fri 10am-8pm,
Sat 9am-6pm, Sun 10am-3.30pm
This small rustic shop offers an interesting
and upmarket range of farmhouse cheeses
from small producers – bestsellers include
Brie de Meaux, with its "mushroomy"
flavour and Montgomery Cheddar. The
shop also stocks "anything which goes with
cheese", ranging from Wendy Brandon
preserves to upmarket breads.
Also at: *32 Earl's Court, W8 (see below)*

Cheeses
11 Fortis Green Road, N10
(020-8-444 9141)
Bus: 134
Open: Tue-Fri 10am-6pm, Sat 9.30am-6pm
Tucked away in an old-fashioned parade of
shops just off Muswell Hill Broadway, this
tiny shop offers an excellent array of
European cheeses, served by friendly and
helpful staff.

La Fromagerie
30 Highbury Park, N5
(020-7-937 8004)
Tube: Highbury & Islington
Open: Mon-Sat 9.30am-7.30pm;
Sun 10am-5pm
Specialist in fine French and Italian cheeses
(see page 62 for more details).

WEST LONDON

Barstow & Barr
32 Earl's Court Road, W8
(020-7-937 8004)
Tube: Earl's Court or High Street Kensington
Open: Mon-Fri 10am-6.30pm; Sat 9am-6pm;
Sun 11am-4pm
(See above for more details)

GENERAL FOODSHOPS

CHOCOLATE

CENTRAL

Charbonnel et Walker
1 The Royal Arcade
28 Old Bond Street, W1
(020-7-491 0939)
Tube: Piccadilly Circus
Open: Mon-Fri 9am-6pm; Sat 10am-5pm
An elegant chocolatiers, established in 1875,
which sells high quality chocolates,
including classic rose and violet creams,
charming novelties and smartly-packaged
chocolate gifts.

Rococo
321 King's Road, SW3
(020-7-352 5857)
Tube: Sloane Square, then the 11, 19 or 22 bus
Open: Mon-Sat 10am-6.30pm

Chocolate lover Chantal Coady (a founder
of the chocolate society) set up this pretty
shop which offers an imaginative range of
goodies (including in-house artisan-made
chocolate bars flavoured with spices and
flowers) and an enticing range of chocolate
novelties.

NORTH

Ackermans
9 Goldhurst Terrace, NW6
(020-7-624 2742)
Tube: Finchley Road
Open: Mon-Fri 9.30am-6pm; Sat 9.30am-5pm
This small, discreet chocolate shop offers a
classic range of homemade chocolates,
including the finest handmade dark
chocolate mint wafers, superior truffles and
pretty novelties.

DELICATESSENS

CENTRAL

Villandry
170 Great Portland Street, W1
(020-7-631 3131)
Tube: Great Portland Street
Open: Mon-Sat 8.30am-10pm; Sun 11am-4pm
Formerly in a picturesque shop on
Marylebone High Street, Jean Charles
Carrarini's distinctive deli-cum-restaurant is
now housed in large, airy premises on Great
Portland Street. Stock (around 50% of
which is organic) is beautifully displayed,
from the baskets of fresh fruit and vegetables
(including black potatoes and elephant
garlic) to the shelves of Legrand wines.
Ample space allows shoppers to wander
round and browse through the goodies:
from homebaked breads and patisserie to
superior cheeses and charcuterie. Jean
Charles also enjoys hunting out delicious
and interesting new foodstuffs for his shop,
ranging from Colzac oil to Jamaican Ginger
Pepper Jelly.

NORTH-WEST

Joy
511 Finchley Road, NW3
(020-7-435 7711)
Tube: Finchley Road
Open: Mon-Fri 9.30am-8pm; Sat 9.30am-7pm
Housed in a old tiled butcher's shop, this is,
in owner Kevin Gould's words, "a kitchen
with a shop". The appetising smell of
roasting chickens testifies to the presence
behind the scenes of 12 kitchen staff, who
produce everything from exquisite raspberry
tarts to traiteur dishes such as Tunisian
mussel soup or chicken with lemons.
Additional delicacies on offer include
handmade harissa sauce from Tunisia, top-
notch olives and nuts, Baker & Spice breads
and good olive oils.

SOUTH-WEST

Mise-en-Place
21 Battersea Rise, SW11
(020-7-228 4392)
BR: Clapham Junction
Mon-Fri 9am-9pm; Sat & Sun 8.30am-7pm
A stylish delicatessen with upmarket stock,
including an extensive range of olives,
French farmhouse cheeses, pastas and
traiteur dishes from the co-owned La Bouffe
restaurant a few doors down.
Also at: *26 The Pavement (020-7-622 4051)*

Mortimer & Bennett
33 Turnham Green Terrace, W4
(020-8-995 4145)
Tube: Turnham Green
Open: Mon-Fri 8.30am-6.30pm;
Sat 8.30am-5.30pm
This small, smartly-tiled shop is crammed
with goodies, from cheeses, salamis and
pâtés, to a range of up to 30 different olive
oils. Sweet treats include Bonnat's
chocolate, Sally Clarke's biscuits and
rumtopf ice-creams.

Vivian's
2 Worple Way, TW10
(020-8-940 3600)
Tube: Richmond
Open: Mon-Fri 9am-7pm; Sat 8.30am-6pm;
Sun 8.30am-12noon
Run with discerning enthusiasm by Vivian
Martin, this immaculate foodshop (with a
pretty Art Nouveau frontage) is an Aladdin's
cave of good things to eat, ranging from
mortadella with truffles to chef Stephen
Bull's pecan pies. The cheese counter
features an excellent range of British, French
and Italian farmhouse cheeses while the fresh
produce comes in weekly from Milan. "I do
like a provenance for everything," explains
Vivian, who actively seeks out and supports
small British producers. She stocks Botton
Village fruit cordials, Wormersley Hall herb
vinegars and Rosebud Farm pickles.

FISHMONGER'S

A. Scott & Son

CENTRAL

Blagden
65 Paddington Street, W1
(020-7-935 8321)
Tube: Baker Street
Open: Mon 7.30am-4.30pm; Tue-Fri
7.30am-5pm; Sat 7.30am-1pm
An eye-catching display of fish and seafood
arrnaged on a marble slab marks this
attractive purpose-built fishmongers that
dates back to 1890. Run with knowledge
and courtesy by Peter and Albert Curd
(who with David Blagden are partners in
the business) it offers an upmarket selection
of quality seafood. scallops in their shell,
fresh Salcombe farm wild salmon, turbot
and halibut. Game and poultry are also on
offer, from grey-leg English partridge to
Kelly bronze free-range turkeys.

Fish!
Cathedral Street, Borough Market, SE1
(020-7-407 3801)
Tube: London Bridge
Open: Mon-Fri 10am-7pm; Sat 10am-4pm
A vision in chrome and glass, this classy
shop is linked to the popular seafood
restaurant next door and prides itself on the
quality and freshness of its seafood which
ranges from organic salmon to brown
shrimps. The fresh fish is served in ready-to-
cook portions, reflecting the restaurant's
daily menu. Other popular items include
fish sausages, homemade fishcakes and a
range of sauces and salsas.

La Maree
76 Sloane Avenue, SW3
(020-7-589 8067)
Tube: South Kensington
Open: Mon-Sat 8am-6pm
This tiny annexe of the Poisonnerie restaurant
offers a small but select range of seafood,
including scallops in their shell and wild
salmon. Prices are high but so is the quality
and the staff are knowledgeable and helpful.

NORTH

B & M Seafoods
258 Kentish Town Road, NW5
(020-7-485 0346)
Tube: Kentish Town
Open: Tue-Sat 9am-6pm
An unpretentious shop, which usefully
combines a butcher's section specialising in
free-range and organic meat with a
fishmonger's.

France Fresh Fish
(see entry on page 27)

Hampstead Seafoods
78 Hampstead High Street, NW3
(020-7-435 3966)
Tube: Hampstead
Open: Tue-Fri 7.30am-5pm;
Sat 7.30am-4.30pm
Tucked away off the High Street, this small
shop offers Hampstead shoppers a good
range of quality seafood.

Steve Hatt
88-90 Essex Road, N1
(020-7-226 3963)
Tube: Angel
Open: Tue-Sat 7am-5pm
An Islington institution, this down-to-earth
fishmonger's has a good range of fish,
stocking everything from herring to
swordfish. The own-smoked fish is very
popular.

Walter Purkis & Sons
17 The Broadway, N8
(020-8-340 6281)
Tube: Finsbury Park, then the W7 bus
Open: Tue-Sat 8am-5pm
Situated on Crouch End's bustling
Broadway, this friendly shop offers a good
range of fish, from herring to salmon.

A. Scott & Son
94 High Road, N2
(020-8-444 7606)
Tube: East Finchley
Open: Tue-Thur 8.30am-5.30pm; Fri
8.30am-6pm; Sat 8.30am-5pm
This small, friendly fishmonger's has an excellent range of fresh fish and seafood, with luxury items including clams, raw tiger prawns and frozen crabmeat. Particularly popular among regulars is the own-smoked fish: undyed haddock and cod and excellent salmon.

SOUTH-EAST

Condon Fishmonger's
363 Wandsworth Road, SW8
(020-7-622 2934)
Tube: Stockwell
Open: Tue-Wed & Fri-Sat 8.45am-5.30pm;
Thur 8.45am-1pm
Ken Condon presides over this down-to-earth fishmonger's, noted for its own-cured smoked fish, from haddock to salmon.

Soper's
141 Evelina Road, SE15
(020-7-639 9729)
BR: Nunhead
Open: Tue-Sat 9am-5.30pm; Sun 9am-2pm
The appropriately-named Whiting family run this classic 'wet fish shop', which has been in the family since 1897. Customers come from a large catchment area to purchase prime, professionally-prepared fish and seasonal extras such as samphire.

EAST

Leadenhall Market
(see entry on page 4)

WEST

Covent Garden Fishmonger's
37 Turnham Green Terrace, W4
(020-8-995 9273)
Tube: Turnham Green
Open: Tue, Wed & Fri 8am-5.30pm;
Thur & Sat 8am-5pm
For a small fishmonger's, Phil Diamond's shop stocks an impressive range of seafood: from fresh wild Scotch salmon to Pallourde clams and langoustine. The 'deli' counter features anchovies in vinaigrette, caviar and sachets of squid ink.

Goldborne Fisheries
75 Goldborne Road, W10
Tube: Ladbroke Grove
(020-8-960 3100)
Open: Mon 9.30am-4pm; Tue-Sat 8am-6pm
George's bustling fish shop is a Portobello institution. Recently expanded nextdoor into a much larger, colourful corner shop, the range of stock is enormous: from live eels and octopuses to tropical fish such as barracuda and parrot fish, and an excellent range of shellfish.

FOOD HALLS

CENTRAL

Bluebird
350 Kings Road, SW3
020-7-559 1000
Tube: Sloane Square
Open: Mon-Wed 9am-8pm;
Thur-Sat 9am-9pm; Sun 12noon-6pm
Conceived on a characteristically grand
scale, Terence Conran's Gastrodrome is
housed in the lovingly-refurbished 1923
Bluebird Garage, and offers everything
from charcuterie and cheeses to fine wines
and fresh seafood. As one would expect,
presentation is stylish, from the Philip
Starck organic groceries to an elegant array
of olive oils. Highlights include the bakery
section which offers 40-50 bread varieties a
day (all made on the premises in wood-
fired ovens), and the butcher's counter,
where bestsellers include beef steak,
marinated chicken and garlic, and black
pepper and chilli sausages. Would-be diners
can choose from a café, a juice bar or an
upstairs restaurant; while the sandwich and
salad bars do a roaring trade at lunchtime.

Fortnum and Mason
181 Piccadilly, W1
(020-7-734 8040)
Tube: Piccadilly Circus
Open: Mon-Sat 9.30am-6pm
With its carpeted floors, pastel-coloured
walls and chandeliers, this famous high-class
grocer's (established in 1707), retains a
certain degree of pomp – and certainly pulls
in the tourists.
Luxuries to be found include Japanese
Gyokura tea (£50 for 125g); wild Irish,
Scotch and English smoked salmon; vintage
whiskies and champagnes; and pheasant's,
partridge's and pullet's eggs.

Harrods
87 Brompton Road, SW1
(020-7-730 1234)
Tube: Knightsbridge
Open: Mon, Tue & Sat 10am-6pm;
Wed-Fri 10am-7pm
The beautiful food halls – some complete
with vintage tiling – remind one of Harrods'
roots as a tea merchant business. With 18
departments, the range of foodstuffs stocked
is enormous: from the eye-catching fresh
fish display to exotic fruits and vegetables.
Highlights include the wide-ranging
charcuterie and cheese counters.

Harvey Nichols Food Hall
Knightsbridge, SW1
(020-7-235 5000)
Tube: Knightsbridge
Open: Mon-Fri 10am-8pm; Sat 10am-6pm
This stylish food hall, with its high-tec
marketplace feel, adjourning restaurant and
smartly-dressed customers, offers an
upmarket range of products focusing on
British foodstuffs. The bakery section and
butcher's and fishmonger's counters are all
impressive. Goods are elegantly packaged in
quintessential Harrods style: a discreet vision
of silver and grey.

Selfridges
400 Oxford Street, W1
(020-7-629 1234)
Tube: Bond Street or Marble Arch
Open: Mon-Wed, Fri & Sat 9.30am-7pm;
Thur 9.30am-8pm
Immaculate and gleaming, the food hall at
Selfridges reflects its cosmopolitan clientele
in its international range of ingredients and
ready-made foods. Particularly impressive is
the long fresh fish counter, with its
eyecatching display of fresh fish and shellfish.

15

HEALTH-FOOD SHOPS

Freshlands

EAST

Freshlands

196 Old Street, EC1
(020-7-250 1708)
Tube: Old Street
Open: Mon-Fri 10.30am-6.30pm;
Sat 10.30am-4.30pm
Bright and light, this large well-established shop attracts a local clientele who are drawn in by helpful staff and an excellent range of organic products. Lunchtimes are particularly busy, as Freshlands' homemade salads and sandwiches make it a popular choice with City workers.

NORTH

Bumblebee

30, 32 & 33 Brecknock Road, N7
(020-7-607 1936)
Tube: Kentish Town, then the 29 bus
Open: Mon-Wed, Fri & Sat 9.30am-6.30pm;
Thur 9.30am-7.30pm
Colonising their particular stretch of Brecknock Road, this trio of busy shops offer an excellent range of health foods, from fresh organic produce to vegetarian cheeses. Staff are very friendly and helpful.

Freshlands

49 Parkway, NW1
(020-7-428 7575)
Tube: Camden Town
Open: Daily 8am-9.30pm
This large, funky shop is very much a New Wave health food shop: it has a juice bar, breakfast bar and Latino music playing in the background. Highlights include the eyecatching display of fresh organic produce and a huge array of self-serve pulses, nuts and dried fruits. The large general stock includes a small organic meat section and freezers filled with organic Rocombe Farm and Green & Black ice creams.

Haelan Centre

41 The Broadway, N8
(020-8-340 4258)
Tube: Finsbury Park, then W7 bus
Open: Mon-Thur 9am-6pm; Fri 12noon-4pm;
Sat 9am-6.30pm
Just by Crouch End's Clock Tower, this corner shop is a local institution. The downstairs shop sells fresh organic produce and health-food groceries ranging from goat's milk to honey; while upstairs there is a health clinic.

Just Natural

304 Park Road, N8
(020-8-340 1720)
Tube Finsbury Park, then the W7 bus
Open: Mon-Sat 9am-7pm; Sun 11am-3pm
Housed in an old, tiled butcher's shop in a pretty parade of shops at the foot of Muswell Hill, this health-food shop's stock is both vegetarian and 100% organic, from the wheatgrass juices and babyfood to the spices and Rocombe Farm ice cream. Staff are friendly and helpful, and an additional plus-point is that mums with buggies are particularly well catered for.

NORTH-WEST

The Realfood Store

14 Clifton Road, W9
(020-7-266 1162)
Tube: Warwick Avenue
Open: Mon-Sat 8am-8pm; Sun 10am-5pm
In a sophisticated take on the traditional health food shop, Kevin Gould's store offers fresh produce (including some organic); a range of excellent nuts, such as lemon-roasted almonds; pulses, honeys, olive oils and upmarket breads. From the kitchen at the back, one can choose from traiteur dishes and homemade pasta sauces, such as rocket pesto.

SOUTH

Brixton Wholefoods Transatlantic
59 Atlantic Road, SW9
(020-7-737 2210)
Tube: Brixton
Open: Mon & Fri 9.30am-6pm;
Tue-Thur & Sat 9.30am-5.30pm
This is a friendly, laid-back wholefood shop, so-named because its former premises were on the other side of Atlantic Road. Organic fruit and veg are delivered three times a week. The self-serve herbs and spices and the range of 20 breads (such as three-seed wholemeal and organic sunflower and sesame) are particularly popular.

SOUTH-WEST

Oliver's Wholefood Store
5 Station Approach, TW9
(020-8-948 3990)
Tube: Kew Gardens
Open: Mon-Sat 9am-7pm; Sun 10am-7pm
This pleasant airy shop has excellent overall stock: from a good range of fresh organic produce (including blood oranges, sweet potatoes and young garlic) which is delivered daily, to neatly arranged shelves of groceries – including organic polenta and rosehip jam. Staff are friendly and helpful and practitioners of complementary medicine come in every week to offer customers free advice.

WEST

Planet Organic
42 Westbourne Grove, W2
(020-7-221 7171)
Tube: Bayswater or Queensway
Open: Mon-Sat 9am-8pm; Sun 11am-5pm
This huge, stylish superstore offers everything for the healthy lifestyle, from freshly-pressed juices at the juice bar to organic muesli. There is a large grocery section, a seafood counter, and a particularly impressive fresh produce section and butcher's counter.

Wild Oats
210 Westbourne Grove, W11
(020-7-229 1063)
Tube: Bayswater or Queensway
Open: Mon-Fri 9am-8pm; Sat 8am-7pm;
Sun 10am-5pm
This large health-food shop (spread over two floors), is a much-loved Notting Hill institution, particularly noted for its friendly and helpful staff. The range of stock is excellent, from an organic fresh produce section, through breads, grains, pastas and condiments to organic wines.

MARKETS

The most exciting recent development on London's food shopping scene is the growing number of new specialist food markets. Borough Market has an enticing range of specialist food stuffs, from fine farmhouse cheeses and breads to continental specialities such as Spanish turron or real balsamic vinegar; and the new Farmers' Market in Islington offers a great chance to buy seasonal foods fresh from the farm – often very competitively priced as no middlemen are involved. Both these markets are proving extremely popular, so come early before the stalls sell out, and bring at least one large bag to carry home all your purchases.

Borough Food Market

Borough Food Market
Tube: London Bridge
Open: The third Saturday of every month,
10am-5pm. There are plans to go weekly.
To find out about market dates contact
Neal's Yard Dairy on 020-7-407 1800.
Housed in Borough's wholesale market
(atmospherically situated under railway
arches next to Southwark Cathedral) and
surrounding side streets, this food market is
growing steadily in popularity.
In an imaginative union, wholesalers – such as
Brindisia (Spanish foodstuffs), Guidetti (Italian
foodstuffs) and Turnips' (quality fruit and
vegetables) – open up to the public, alongside
Borough's local food shops: Fish!, Konditor &
Cook and Neal's Yard Dairy – and a growing
number of other foodshops and producers
who set up stalls specially for the market.
Thus you can buy coffee from the
Monmouth Coffee Company, great breads
from & Clarke's and smoked eel from Brown
& Forest – to name but a few options.

Islington Farmers' Market
Camden Passage, N1
Tube: Angel
Open: Sun 10am-4pm
Founded by Nina Planck, who was inspired
by farmers' markets in her native America,
this market features around 20 farmers who
are all based within 100 miles of London.
Goods on offer range from elderflowers and
pea shoots to really fresh free-range eggs,
goat's cheese, and fruit juices such as pear
and quince.

Spitalfields Organic Market
Commercial Street, E1
Tube: Liverpool Street
Open: Sun 9.30am-5pm
London's first 'organic' market draws a
steady stream of devoted regulars. There is a
lot to attract them, with organic fruit and
veg, farm fresh organic meat, health foods
and the recent addition of a wonderful
German baker's.

TEA & COFFEE

CENTRAL

Algerian Coffee Store
52 Old Compton Street, W1
(020-7-437 2480)
Tube: Leicester Square
Open: Mon-Sat 9am-7pm
A vintage Soho institution, set up in 1887 by
an Algerian businessman and now Italian-
run. The aromatic scent of coffee and spices
wafts out of the door – a clue to the
extensive range of coffees and teas inside.

Angelucci's
(See page 78)

H. R. Higgins
79 Duke Street, W1
(020-7-629 3913)
Tube: Bond Street
Open: Mon-Wed 8.45am-5.30pm;
Thur & Fri 8.45am-6pm; Sat 10am-5pm
Founded in 1942 by Harold Higgins (known
as 'the coffee man'), this family-run business
continues to sell quality teas and coffees. The
huge copper caddies, beautiful old scales and
knowledgeable, courteous service provide a
glimpse into another retail era.

Monmouth Coffee Company
27 Monmouth Street, WC2
(020-7-836 5272)
Tube: Covent Garden
Open: Mon-Sat 9am-6.30pm
With its high-backed tasting booths and
aromatic scent of coffee, this small coffee
shop-cum-café is a much-loved Covent
Garden institution. It offers a discerning
range of carefully-sourced coffee, sold
whole or freshly ground, as requested.

William Martyn

Founder of W. Martyns
~1897

NORTH

SPICES

W. M. Martyn
135 Muswell Hill Broadway, N10
(020-8–883 5642)
Bus: 134
Open: Mon–Wed & Fri 9.30am–5.30pm;
Thur 9.30am–1pm; Sat 9am–5.30pm
The aroma of freshly-roasted coffee beans
wafting down the Broadway marks the
presence of this small, old-fashioned
grocer's, which was established over 100
years ago. While best-known for its teas and
coffees, the shop also stocks a range of
traditional groceries, ranging from excellent
dried fruits to sugar mice and bars of
German marzipan. Staff are helpful and
friendly.

Greencades
No5 The Apprentice Shop
Merton Abbey Mills, South Wimbledon, SW19
(020-8-543 0519)
Tube: Colliers Wood
Open: Daily 9.30am-5.30pm
A large shop offering fresh and dried herbs
of all kinds from basil to more exotic
ingredients such as lemongrass. Greencades
also stock their own range of spices and
seasonings including a wonderful range of
mullling spices.

The Spice Shop
1 Blenheim Crescent, W11
(020-7-221 4448)
Tube: Ladbroke Grove
Open: Mon-Sat 9.30am-6.30pm;
Sun 11am-5pm
Birgit Erath runs this small, aromatic shop
with enormous enthusiasm and energy,
stocking spices and herbs for both culinary
and medicinal purposes.

21

AFRICAN & CARIBBEAN LONDON

Brixton Market

In his monumental book, *Staying Power*, Peter Fryer points out that the first Black presence in Britain dates back to Roman times, when Black men were among the conscripts in the Roman army. The growth of a domestic Black community, however, was connected with Britain's slave trade, which was started in 1562-3 by the first 'triangular voyage' between Britain, Africa and the West Indies. The demand for sugar and the labour-intensive sugar cane plantation system in the Caribbean encouraged the slave trade's growth, making it enormously profitable to those running it.

Africans came to Britain as slaves until the slave trade was outlawed in 1807. Before this date some free Blacks, such as seamen, servants and street entertainers were established in Britain, with the London community living mainly along the Thames in Limehouse. But records such as that of freed slave Ukawsaw Gronniosaw, give a vivid picture of ill-treatment and discrimination, which forced many into destitution. After 1807 the Black community in Britain declined, although Black loyalists returned after fighting in the American War of Independence, and some seamen settled after serving in the Napoleonic Wars (1792-1815). In the late nineteenth century a small community of Somali seamen settled in the London docks.

The coming of the First World War meant a change of attitude towards the Black community. Instead of being rejected for work on racial grounds, their help was now needed in the munitions factories. Black seamen also filled the gaps in the Merchant Navy caused by conscription. By 1919, there were 20,000 Black people in Britain. But once the war was over the picture changed again, with the seamen's unions closing the door firmly against any Black labour.

A similar pattern occurred in the late 1940s and 1950s when, as Britain struggled to rebuild its war-torn economy, a call went out to the Commonwealth for workers to come to the 'Mother Country'. The 1948 Nationality Act granted British citizenship to people living in Britain's current and former colonies. For many West Indians this was an opportunity to be seized; unemployment was high in the West Indies and in 1951 a hurricane added to Jamaica's problems. Corporations such as London Transport actively recruited labour in Barbados in 1956, and by 1966 had also turned to Trinidad and Jamaica. Between 1945 and 1958, over 125,000 West Indians emigrated to Britain.

The different stages of African immigration into London in the post-war years have been triggered by the ebb and flow of African Politics. The 1950s and 1960s saw an influx of West Africans made up largely of students and lawyers. During the 1970s, African and Asian Ugandans fled Idi Amin; while recent years have seen an increase in immigration from Ghana, Zaire and Ethiopia.

There is no single centre for the African community in London, with pockets of different African nationalities scattered throughout the capital. There are, however, focal points such as Brixton and Notting Hill for the West Indian community. Many of the first post-war Jamaican immigrants who sailed over on the Empire Windrush settled in Brixton, a formerly prosperous suburb which had become cheap and run-down. This community attracted further Jamaican immigrants during the 1950s and 1960s. Notting Hill, in which mainly Trinidadians settled, hosts the famous Carnival; what originated as a 1964 Bank Holiday street party for local children has since developed into Europe's largest open-air street festival. The costume parades and rhythmic steel drums all derive from Trinidad's own spectacular Carnival.

AFRICAN & CARIBBEAN CUISINE

'African food' is a blanket term covering a huge number of countries with their own characteristic cuisines. Certain staples, such as maize, cassava, plaintain and beans, are shared across different African countries and crop up in Black cuisine in many parts of the world. Dried foods, such as smoked or salted fish and meat, are another common element in the African kitchen, reflecting the need to preserve food before the days of refrigeration or canning. Many of these ingredients are now used to add a distinctive flavour to dishes.

West African slaves brought their cuisine to the West Indies and its influence is still marked in today's Caribbean cooking. Many of the staples are the same (several brought from Africa): cassava, yams, taro, plaintain, groundnuts. Dishes in common include coo-coo (cornmeal pudding) and fufu, the latter being a Fanti word used on the Cape Coast. In West Africa fufu is pounded yam, plaintain and cassava dough dipped into a soup, while in Jamaica fufu now means both the pounded yam and the soup. The slaves' restricted diet also included salted meat and fish and these are still popular, although the latter is now something of a luxury.

Caribbean cooking is very much a melting pot of a cuisine, influenced by a series of colonisers and immigrants. Chillies were brought from South America by the Spanish colonisers and 'escovished fish', fresh pickled fish, originated from the Spanish dish escabeche. The arrival in Trinidad of indentured workers from India means that dishes like roti and curry goat are popular there today; a large proportion of the island's inhabitants have Indian roots.

The fertility of the Caribbean islands meant many plants could be introduced successfully. Staples now include breadfruit, which was introduced by Captain Bligh. Fresh seafood is characteristic of West Indian cuisine and increasingly fish such as colourful snappers are becoming available in Britain.

GLOSSARY

Ackee: a red-skinned fruit that is only safe to eat when the fruit is fully ripe. The white, fleshy base called an aril is the part that is eaten. Fresh ackee is very rarely found but it is available in tins. Saltfish with ackee is one of Jamaica's famous dishes. The Latin name of the fruit, *Blighia sapida*, is a tribute to Captain Bligh, who introduced it to Jamaica.

Agbono: sometimes spelt ogbono, this is the inner kernel of the African bush mango. The kernel is the size and shape of an almond but browner and much harder. Available both whole and ground.

Allspice: peppercorn-sized berries, with a flavour that combines cloves, cinnamon and nutmeg – hence the name.

Annatto: small, orange-red seeds, used to add colour and flavour.

Arrowroot: a starch extracted from the underground stem of a water-plant.

Avocado: this green-skinned, soft-fleshed fruit is called 'pear' in the Caribbean.

Bananas: green bananas, which are the unripe fruit of certain varieties, and ripe yellow bananas are treated as both a vegetable and a fruit in Caribbean and African cuisines.

Bitter leaf: A distinctively flavoured African leaf, related to the lettuce family. Available dried or frozen.

Breadfruit: a football-sized fruit with thick, green, pimply skin and creamy flesh, used both as a starchy vegetable and in pies and puddings.

Callaloo: green leaves of the dasheen plant, used to make a famous eponymous soup. Available tinned and fresh.

Cassava: large, brown, hand-shaped tubers of the cassava plant, also called manioc or yucca. Bitter cassava, despite the fact it contains toxic prussic acid which must be removed by either cooking or pressing, is a staple food. Yellow-fleshed sweet cassava is eaten as a vegetable. Dried, ground cassava is used in Africa to make gari. Ground cassava meal is used in the West Indies to make a type of bread and the flavoured juice of grated cassava is used to make cassareep, a key ingredient of pepperpot.

Catfish, dried: small blackened fish, with a distinctive large head, used to add flavour to soups and stews in West African cooking.

Cho-cho (christophene, chayote): a pear-sized member of the squash family, with a wrinkled skin ranging in colour from white to green, and watery white flesh.

Coconut: coconut flesh and milk are widely used in Caribbean cookery.

Cornmeal: coarsely or finely ground dried corn kernels.

Crayfish, dried: although called 'crayfish' in Africa, these are a type of shrimp. Used whole or ground as flavouring.

Custard apple: apple-sized fruit with a knobbly, green skin. The white, sweet pulp has a custard-like texture, hence the name.

Dasheen: potato-sized fibrous tubers with white starchy flesh. Some varieties of dasheen have an acrid taste.

Eddoe: a small, rounded fibrous tuber with white starchy flesh.

Peppers

Egusi: pumpkin seeds, which are available shelled, either whole or ground. Egusi is used in West African cooking, providing a nutty texture in soups and stews.

Fish: flying fish, a distinctive 'winged' fish; king fish, a firm-fleshed 'meaty' fish, often sold as steaks; parrot fish, a brightly-coloured fish with a beaky head; snapper, a popular, firm-fleshed fish, available in colours from grey to pinkish-red; and trevalli, a large, firm-fleshed oily fish. Jacks is the name given to the smaller fish of the same family.

Gari: coarsely-ground cassava, an African staple.

Guava: small, yellow-green, hard-skinned fruit with pinkish flesh filled with small seeds. It has a distinctive fragrance and is eaten raw or used to make jams and jellies.

Guinep: small, round, green fruit which grows in bunches. The pink flesh has a delicate flavour.

Irish moss: white, curly seaweed from which an eponymous drink is made. Available either dried or drinkable form.

Jackfruit: a large, green fruit with a pimply skin, similar in appearance to breadfruit.

Kenke: West African dumpling, made from fermented maize flour wrapped in corn husks or banana leaves and cooked.

Landsnails: giant snails, sold either alive, frozen, tinned or smoked. If bought alive, keep them and feed them for a few days before cooking to make sure they have excreted anything toxic.

Mango: this large, kidney-shaped fruit, with its succulent orange flesh and sweet, resiny flavour, comes in numerous varieties. One of the best-known West Indian varieties is the Julie mango.

Okra (ladies fingers, ochroes): finger-sized, ridged, tapering green pods, introduced into the Caribbean from West Africa.

Ortanique: a cross between an orange and a tangerine, this looks like an orange with a flattened end.

Palm hearts: tender palm tree hearts, usually found tinned.

Palm oil: a thick, orange-red oil, made from the fruit of the oil palm, which adds flavour and colour to African dishes.

Pawpaw: long, oval fruit, with soft orange flesh, varying in skin colour from green to orange.

Peppers: among the hottest and most flavourful of the peppers used in African and Caribbean cooking is the squat, rounded Scotch bonnet pepper, available in green, yellow and red varieties.

Pepper sauce: the sauce comes in a variety of textures from liquid to paste, but is always hot!

Pigeon pea (gunga): ridged pea pods, with every pea in its own section. Unusually, the peas within a single pod vary in colour from cream through green and brown. Available fresh, tinned or dried.

Plaintain: similar in appearance to green bananas, plaintain have starchy flesh and are cooked and eaten as a vegetable. They can be chipped, boiled or cooked in stews.

Pomelo: often called shaddock, after the merchant ship captain who introduced the fruit to the Caribbean, this is a large, thick-skinned citrus fruit, similar in flavour to grapefruit.

Saltfish: preserved foods such as salted fish were brought over to the Caribbean to feed the plantation workers. It is now something of a luxury item. Stockfish is a popular salted fish.

Sapodilla (naseberry): a fruit very similar in appearance to kiwi fruit, with a brown, furry skin. Inside it has pinky-brown, granular flesh with a few glossy pips and a distinctive sweet flavour.

Sorrel (rosella): the red sepals of a flowering plant, used either fresh or dried to make a dark-red, aromatic drink, traditionally at Christmas.

Soursop: a large, oval-shaped fruit with a thick, green, spiny skin. The pinkish-white flesh inside is custard-textured with a delicate, tart flavour.

Sugar cane: similar in appearance to bamboo, this plant has played a considerable part in Caribbean history as the sugar cane plantations demanded extensive labour, provided by slaves. Short lengths of the woody stalk are either chewed and sucked for their sweet refreshing juice.

Sweet potato: a sweet-fleshed tuber, available in many varieties.

Yam: a family of large, brown-skinned, starchy tubers, which come in many varieties, both yellow and white-fleshed.

FOODSHOPS

AFRICAN & CARIBBEAN LONDON

L ively markets lined with fruit, vegetable and fish stalls are characteristic food shopping centres for the African and Caribbean community. For meat halal butcher's are used ('halal' describes meat from animals killed in convention with Muslim law), with many offering West Indian cuts in addition to their normal range.

EAST

Queens Market
Green Street, E7 (on the corner of Queen Road)
Open: Tue & Thur-Sat 8am-5pm
Tube: Upton Park
Among the clothing and household goods are a number of stalls and shops selling Caribbean foodstuffs, such as the fish stall with its tilapia and snapper and the halal butcher's around the edge of the market.

Ridley Road Market
Ridley Road, E8
BR: Dalston Junction
Open: Tue–Sat 9am–5pm
A large, bustling market with a mixture of English and West Indian fruit and vegetable stalls, fishmonger's and halal butcher's, mixed in with fabric and hair-care stalls.

NORTH

The stretch of Stroud Green Road nearest to Finsbury Park tube station is home to a number of African and Caribbean foodshops, ranging from greengrocer's to halal butcher's.

France Fresh Fish
99 Stroud Green Road, N4
(020-7–263 9767)
Tube: Finsbury Park
Open: Mon-Sat 9am-7pm
A tropical fish specialist, linked to the well-known Mauritian fish restaurant next door, which sells a colourful selection of seafood, including barracuda, conch and parrot fish.

Mehboob
35 Stroud Green Road, N4
(020-7–263 7654)
Tube: Finsbury Park
Open: Mon–Sat 9am-8pm; Sun 10am–6pm
A well-established food shop, run with relaxed friendliness, which stocks both West Indian and African foodstuffs, including Ghanaian smoked fish, a range of flours and fresh vegetables and fruit.

K. M. Butcher's Grocer's
29 Stroud Green Road, N4
(020-7-263 6625)
Tube: Finsbury Park
Open: Mon-Sat 8am-8.30pm; Sun 9am-7pm
A large store, complete with a counter piled high with goat's meat and chickens, and groceries ranging from Mauby syrup drinks to bags of cornmeal.

Stroud Green Food Store
65 Stroud Green Road, N4
(020-7–272 0348)
Tube: Finsbury Park
Open: Mon–Sun 8am–8pm
A neatly-arranged store with an attractive display of fresh fruit and vegetables outside, including breadfruit, mangoes, plaintain and bunches of thyme.

SOUTH

Brixton Market
Brixton Station Road, Pope's Road, Atlantic Road, Electric Road and Electric Avenue
Tube: Brixton
Open: Mon, Tue & Thur-Sat 8am-5.30pm; Wed 8am-1pm
This is the best market in London for West Indian and African foodstuffs. Spread out through streets and arcades alongside a mixture of household goods, wig and fabric shops are a range of colourful fruit and vegetable stalls, fishmonger's and butcher's – some of them with signs advertising 'meat so tender you don't need teeth'! Saturday is the busiest market day and the noise is tremendous: music blaring from the record shops and people exchanging greetings, catching up on news and arguing over prices. Below are a few shops I have picked out, but this is a place to explore and discover bargains for yourself.

Back Home Foods
83, 1st Avenue, Granville Arcade
A huge corner greengrocer's shop, selling a good selection of fruit and vegetables such as plaintain and sugar cane, as well as a range of African ingredients like egusi.

Dagon's
16, 1st Avenue, Granville Arcade
A well-established and popular fishmonger's which, despite limited space, stocks a range of fish including jackfish, snappers and catfish.

Ghana House
27-28, 3rd Avenue, Granville Arcade
As the name suggests, this shop specialises in West African foodstuffs including dried fish.

WEST

Portobello Road Market
Portobello Road, W12
Tube: Notting Hill Gate
Open: Mon-Sat 9am-5pm
Past the antique shops is a lively fruit and vegetable market. Several of the stalls here sell West Indian produce such as yams, Scotch Bonnet peppers and okra.

Shepherd's Bush Market
Uxbridge Road, W12
Tube: Goldhawk Road or Shepherd's Bush
Open: Mon-Wed, Fri & Sat 9am-5pm; Thur 9am-1pm
A decade ago this was a larger, more food-orientated market. Alongside the fabric, clothing and kitchenware stalls, there are, however, still stalls which sell West Indian fruit and vegetables.

MAIL ORDER

Gramma's Pepper Sauce
PO Box 218
East Ham
London E6 4BG
(020-8-470 8751)
Dawn Moore produces the best and hottest pepper sauce I have ever tried. She will supply jars of mild, medium and super-hot pepper sauce.

EATING PLACES

CENTRAL

Calabash £££
The Africa Centre
38 King Street, WC2
(020-7-836 1976)
Tube: Covent Garden
This basement restaurant offers a range of reasonably priced dishes from around Africa.

NORTH

Bee Wees £££
96 Stroud Green Road, N4
(020-7-263 4004)
Tube: Finsbury Park
This relaxed restaurant, famous for its rum punch, is a Stroud Green institution and serves up delicious dishes.

Cottons Rhum Shop
Bar & Restaurant £££
55 Chalk Farm Road, NW1
(020-7-482 1096)
Tube: Chalk Farm
Popular with parties making merry, this is an atmospheric establishment serving Caribbean classics like jerk chicken.

Humming Bird £££
84 Stroud Green Road, N4
(020-7-263 9690)
Tube: Finsbury Park
A pleasant restaurant offering a good cross-section of food including Caribbean classics such as crab callaloo.

SOUTH

Smokey Joe's Diner £££
131 Wandsworth High Street, SW18
(020-8-871 1785)
Tube: East Putney
A relaxed, unpretentious Caribbean restaurant which is hugely popular.

WEST

Mandola £££
139 Westbourne Grove, W11
Tube: Bayswater or Queensway
This small, relaxed Sudanese restaurant, run with great charm by Yusuf and his wife, serves tasty food such as salata aswad (aubergine salad) and kustalata (lamb cutlets) at remarkably reasonable prices. Round off your meal with the delectable date mousse and traditional Sudanese coffee. Its fame has spread and booking is recommended, especially at weekends.

COOKBOOKS

Caribbean and African Cookery
Rosamund Grant
An informative and readable cookbook.

Caribbean Cooking
Elizabeth Lambert Ortiz
An excellent look at Caribbean cuisine.

Creole Caribbean Cookery
Kenneth Gardiner
A well-written cookbook.

Nigerian Cookbook
H.O. Anthonio and M. Isoun
A very clear and informative book.

A Taste of Africa
Dorinda Hafner
A fascinating look at African and Caribbean cookery, written with exuberance and infectious enthusiasm.

Trade Wind: Caribbean Cooking
Christine Mackie
An evocative mix of text and recipes.

AFRICAN & CARIBBEAN LONDON

29

ASIAN LONDON

Ealing Road, Wembley

T he term 'Asian' covers what was once the Indian subcontinent but is today, Bangladesh, India, Pakistan and Sri Lanka. An Asian presence in Britain can be traced back to the seventeenth and eighteenth centuries. Some early settlers were performers but many were servants brought back from India by the newly prosperous nawabs. Through the East India Company others came as lascars, Indian seamen.

A fascinating book, *Across Seven Seas* (edited by Caroline Adams), describes how many of these lascars were from one small, land-locked part of Bengal called Sylhet. There was a tradition in rural India of men leaving their villages to work and support their family. Work as seamen was offered at large ports such as Calcutta. In the words of Haji Kona Miah: 'The Sylhet people were in the ship because these people follow each other, and some went there and others saw them and thought they could get jobs too'. The serangs, agents who chose workers for the ships, preferred to employ people from their own village or locality. Once Sylhetis became serangs, a pattern of using Sylheti sailors was established.

Those who settled in London lived in the East End, near the docks. For many of them earning a living was difficult; in 1858 the 'Strangers Home for Asiatics, Africans and South Sea Islanders' was opened in West India Dock Road, Limehouse. The major growth in the Bengali community came this century in 1956, when passports were finally granted and thousands of people came to London. By 1962, the number of Bengali immigrants living in the East End had swelled from approximately 300 to 5,000.

Of course, it was not only Bengali seamen who came to London: doctors, politicians and lawyers were also among the immigrants. Indeed, three men pivotal to India's independence studied law in London at the turn of the century: Mohandas Karamchand (later Mahatma) Gandhi, Mohammed Ali Jinnah and Jawaharlal Nehru. In 1892 Dabadhai Naoroji, a campaigner for Indian rights, was elected as Britain's first Asian MP by a majority of three votes.

It was in the period following the Second World War that the Asian presence in Britain expanded considerably; the 1948 Nationality Act granted the right of British citizenship to Britain's colonies and former colonies. After Indian Independence the violent partition of India and Pakistan left thousands dispossessed. Britain officially encouraged mainly unskilled workers from India and Pakistan to come to Britain and by 1958 there were around 55,000 Asians in Britain. The next wave of immigration came in the late 1960s when Asians were expelled from Uganda, and in 1972, when Idi Amin expelled nearly 30,000 Ugandan Asians who arrived in Britain within the space of three months.

The Asian community today, like the complex Indian subcontinent, is made up of people from different countries who speak different languages and practice different faiths. Certain areas in London are linked to particular groups. Brick Lane, which over the centuries has housed different waves of immigrants, is now predominantly Bengali, the Sylhet seamen who first settled there having paved the way for others. The history of Brick Lane is encapsulated in the story of one building on Fournier Street: built as a Huguenot chapel in 1774, it later became a Methodist chapel; in 1898 it was converted into a Jewish synagogue, and nowadays it functions as the London Jamme Masjid mosque.

Wembley is a Gujarati area, while Southall is predominantly Punjabi and Sikh. There are various theories about Southall's roots. One is that workers brought out to construct the new airport at Heathrow settled near their worksite. Alternatively, it is thought that work was provided for Asian labourers in local factories and the community grew up around this. Southall today is a thriving community with everything from Sikh temples to bookshops and restaurants. London's Hindu community, meanwhile, is justly proud of 'Shri Swaminarayan Mandir' (020-8-965 2651), the traditional Hindu temple recently built in Neasden. The gleaming white marble temple, which rises like a mirage in an urban setting just off the North Circular, is unique in Europe as an example of traditional Indian temple construction. It is made from blocks of limestone and marble which were hand-carved in India then shipped over and assembled in London. There is an adjourning Haveli (community centre) decorated with intricate wooden carvings – visitors to the temple complex are courteously welcomed.

ASIAN CUISINE

The term 'Indian cuisine' is a catch-all phrase, covering the diverse cuisines of India, Pakistan, Bangladesh and Sri Lanka – and a huge spectrum of regional, religious and cultural differences. The hallmark of all Indian cuisine is the emphasis on spices and herbs. These numerous flavourings, from aromatic crocus stamens (saffron) to pungent resin (asafoetida), are used in intricate and varying ways: dry-roasted, fried in hot oil or mixed with other spices to form a masala (spice mix). Underlying their culinary use is an ancient belief in the health-giving properties of spices. In the Holy Hindu Scriptures, Ayurvedic scripts list the medicinal properties of herbs and spices. Turmeric and cloves both have antiseptic properties. Asafoetida, a digestive which prevents flatulence, is added to lentil dishes. Spices are divided into 'warm', generating internal heat, and 'cool', lessening it. Warm spices, such as black cardamom and nutmeg, are used in winter dishes.

Underneath this culinary umbrella are diverse cuisines influenced by religion (the main Indian faiths being Hinduism, Islam, Buddhism, Jainism and Sikhism), geography and culture. Religions have laid down rules and taboos as to what can or cannot be eaten. For example, the Hindus will not eat beef as the cow (tended by Lord Krishna in myth) is a sacred animal. Some Hindus are vegetarian, while for strict vegetarians even the flavourings associated with meat (garlic and onion) are forbidden in cooking. For Muslims, pork is a forbidden meat.

When describing Indian cuisine in regional terms, it is possible to draw a crude north-south boundary, although there are exceptions. Flat wheat breads such as paratha and chapati are a staple in the north while rice is the staple in the south. Northern cuisine was influenced by Mogul rulers who came down to India through Persia and brought with them many of the dishes we now consider typical of Indian cuisine. The Persian influence is apparent in the subtle spicing, the use of nuts and in dishes such as pullao, a descendant of the pilaff. From this luxurious court cuisine came techniques used today: korma (braising in a thick, often nut-based sauce); pot-roasting (in a traditional charcoal stove); and kebab, kofte and tandoori (dishes cooked in a tandoor oven). The Indian food that is most frequently served in restaurants both within and outside India is based on this Mogul cuisine. In Southern Indian cookery the coconut palm has an influential role, with sweet coconut milk used in many dishes. Rice is eaten not just as a grain but is ground, mixed with dal, and used to make light pancakes called dosai. A similar mix, when fermented, is used to make spongy, tangy cakes called idlee. As in other hot climates, fermentation is a well-used culinary technique.

GLOSSARY

Angled loofah: a green gourd with distinctive raised ridges running down its length and a bitter flavour.

Asafoetida (heeng): a pungent brown resin, valued for its digestive properties, sold in either lump or powder form.

Bitter gourd (karela): a knobbly-skinned, cucumber-shaped green gourd with a distinctive bitter flavour and digestive properties.

Bottle gourd (dudi): a large, smooth, bottle-shaped, green-skinned gourd with marrow-like flesh.

Cardamom: a fragrant spice pod sold whole, hulled or ready-ground. The small green or white cardamoms are used in both sweet and savoury dishes while the larger wrinkled black cardamom is used only in savoury dishes.

Carom (ajwan): a tiny seed spice, like miniature fennel seeds, with a medicinal scent and sharp, thyme-like flavour.

Chayote (chow-chow): A pear-sized, wrinkled, green-skinned squash with a single large seed and marrow-like flesh.

Chenna: a ricotta-like curd cheese.

Chick–pea flour (gram or besan): ground chickpeas are the basis for many breads and fritters. Madhur Jaffrey recommends storing it in the fridge.

Chick–peas (channa): fresh chickpeas are small, puffy green pods which need peeling to reveal the kernel.

Chikoo (sapodilla): similar in appearance to kiwi fruit with a fine brown, furry skin, pinky-brown granular flesh, a few glossy pips and a distinctive sweet flavour.

Chikoo

Chillies: sold both fresh and dried. Long slim green chillies and dried red chillies are used in Indian cookery to add both pungent heat and a distinctive flavour.

Chilli powder: a hot red powder made from ground, dried red chillies.

Cluster beans (guar): fine, straight green beans.

Coconut milk: a thick white liquid made from grated coconut flesh and not, as is sometimes thought, from the cloudy liquid inside the coconut which is called 'coconut water'. Homemade coconut milk can be made by blending together dessicated coconut with hot water, then sieving it. Alternatively, tinned coconut milk is a convenient, ready-to-use product – Madhur Jaffrey recommends the Chaokoh brand. Creamed coconut or coconut milk powder needs diluting before use.

Ghee

Coriander: both the aromatic green leaves (similar in appearance to flat-leafed parsley) and small rounded seeds are used extensively in Indian cookery.

Cumin: small, greenish, finely-ridged oval seeds, similar to caraway seeds, with a distinctive, slightly sharp flavour, widely used in Indian cookery. Black cumin, which is rarer, has a more pronounced herbal flavour.

Curry leaf: a spicy-smelling leaf which resembles a small bay leaf. It's usually sold dried but sometimes branches of fresh curry leaves are available.

Dal: a generic term covering the three types of pulses (lentils, beans and peas) used in Indian cookery: chana dal, small yellow split peas; masoor dal, tiny pink split lentils (sometimes called red split lentils); moong dal, yellow split mung beans (sold both skinned and unskinned); rajma dal, red kidney beans; toovar dal, a large split yellow pea; urad dal, ivory-coloured hulled black gram beans (used in Southern Indian vegetarian cookery in dishes such as pancakes and fried dumplings).

Drumsticks: long, green, ridged pods with a thick skin, fibrous pulp and a distinctive flavour. Usually available tinned but sometimes found fresh.

Fennel: aniseed-flavoured, greenish ridged seeds, valued as a digestive. Candied fennel seeds are eaten after a meal.

Fenugreek (methi): both the small, stubby, hard, yellow seeds and the spicy-smelling, bitter green leaves are used in Indian cookery. The seeds have a strong, bitter flavour and are used in pickles. The dark green trefoil leaves, which look similar to clover, are sold both fresh and dried.

Fish: hilsa, a prized freshwater fish from Bangladesh; pomfret, a flat, round-shaped and white-fleshed fish.

Garam masala: a fragrant spice mix, available in many versions.

Ghee: clarified butter with a nutty flavour. Because of the clarification, ghee can be used for deep frying and stored at room temperature.

Ginger: this knobbly, light-brown root is a key flavouring prized for its aromatic flavour and digestive qualities.

Guava: a fruit resembling a small, knobbly pear, with a distinctive aroma, pinkish flesh and several small, hard seeds.

Hyacinth bean (seim): a broad-podded, thick-skinned, curved green bean; a member of the hyacinth bean family.

Jackfruit: a huge fruit with a thick, green studded skin. The creamy-textured flesh inside is eaten as a vegetable when unripe and as a fruit when ripe.

Jaggery: a pale brown sugar with a rich, nutty flavour, made from sugar cane juice or palm sap, and used in Indian sweets.

Kohlrabi: a pale green or purple bulbous vegetable, resembling a sprouting turnip – but with a more delicate flavour.

Kokum: an inedible variety of mangosteen, sold in dried pieces and used as a souring agent.

Lemon crystals: light-coloured crystals used as a souring agent.

Mango: a kidney-shaped fruit, with succulent orange flesh and a sweet, resiny flavour, which is enormously popular in India. Tart, green unripe mangoes are used to make pickles, chutneys and relishes while orange-red ripe mangoes are eaten on their own or used in desserts. Over a thousand varieties are grown in India, but the Alphonso mango is one of the best known in Britain.

Mango powder (amchoor): sour, beige-coloured powder made from dried, unripe mangoes, used to add a tart flavour to food.

Mustard oil: a pungent yellow oil, made from mustard seeds, used extensively in northern India and Bangladesh.

Mustard seeds: tiny, black round seeds, often used in pickles.

Okra (bhindi, ladies fingers): a tapering, ridged green pod which exudes a sticky juice when cooked.

Onion seed (kalonji or nigella): tiny tear-shaped black seeds which, despite their name, are not related to onions. Used primarily in pickles but also on tandoori naan bread.

Panch phoran: a Bengali five-spice mix, containing cumin, fennel, onion seeds, fenugreek and black mustard seeds.

Paneer: a firm white cheese, made from pressed Indian curd cheese called chenna (which is similar to ricotta).

Patra: large, green taro leaves which are spread with a gram flour paste, rolled and steamed to make a dish called 'patra'.

Phalooda (falooda): transparent, thread-like noodles made from wheatberry starch and flavoured with pine or rose essence, used in desserts, to garnish kulfi or in a drink of the same name.

Pistachio: green-fleshed, delicately-flavoured nuts, used in Indian sweetmeats and ice cream or as a nibble.

Pomegranate seeds (anardana): dried pomegranate kernels, used to add sourness.

Poppadums (papar): small round wafers made from split-peas and flavoured with garlic or spices. When fried in hot oil they puff up and become crispy.

Poppy seed (khas khas): minuscule white poppy seeds, used in ground form to thicken sauces.

Rice: the most famous and expensive of rice varieties grown in India is basmati, with its nutty aroma and flavour.

Rose essence: a delicate rose-scented essence used in desserts. Rose water is a diluted form of rose essence.

Saffron: the dried stigmas of a crocus variety, sold in both thread and powdered form.

Sevian: fine golden-brown wheat vermicelli, used in desserts.

Snake gourd: as the name suggests, a long, narrow, twisted green gourd with bland marrow-like flesh.

Spiny bitter gourd (kantola): a small, spiky, egg-shaped relation of the bitter gourd.

Sweetmeats: many Indian sweetmeats are made from milk boiled down slowly until it thickens (rabadi) or until it takes on a fudge-like consistency (khoya). Varieties include: barfi, a crumbly Indian fudge often flavoured with nuts; gulub jamun, deep-fried dumplings in syrup; halwa: nuts, fruits and vegetables cooked with ghee and sugar to a firm texture; jalebi: bright orange, crisp batter squiggles filled with syrup; kulfi, ice cream made from slow-cooked milk which gives a slightly grainy texture; and rasmalai: delicate, soft chenna dumplings served in rabadi (slow-cooked milk).

Tamarind: a brown fleshy pod with a sour-sweet flavour, used as a souring agent. Both tamarind pulp and tamarind paste are available.

Taro: the term applies to a whole range of fibrous tubers, recognisable by their brown hairy skins and white starchy flesh.

Tinda: a small, rounded member of the marrow family, with pale green skin and white flesh.

Tindola (tindori): walnut-sized 'ivy' gourds with variegated markings and a crisp, crunchy texture.

Turmeric (haldi): a small-fingered, orange-fleshed root from which comes the powdered yellow spice powder of the same name.

Vark: fine edible foil, made from ground silver or gold, used to adorn dishes on special occasions.

White radish (mooli): long, thick white radish, with a mild flavour, used to stuff parathas in Pakistani cooking.

Yard-long beans: exceedingly long, thin green beans.

Yogurt: traditionally made from buffalo milk, Julie Sahni suggests stirring a little soured cream into normal yogurt to reproduce the necessary tangy flavour.

FOODSHOPS

T he range of stock in Asian foodshops is huge, from fresh fruits and vegetables to staples like dals and flours. Often the emphasis is on bulk-buying and stocking up with large sacks of basmati or huge packets of spices. Both Southall and Wembley have this kind of shop, sandwiched amongst stores selling alluring fabric and glittering jewellery. These shops often have a paan counter (a digestive made from shredded betel nut rolled up in a paan leaf).

CENTRAL

Tucked away behind Euston Station, the quiet backwater of Drummond Street is home to a number of excellent, good value Indian restaurants, and a few food shops.

Ambala
112 Drummond Street, NW1
(020-7-387 7886/3521)
Tube: Euston
Open: Mon-Sun 9am-9pm
Ambala have been selling Asian sweets since 1965, when their first small shop opened on this site. Ambala is now a thriving chain and the original shop has been revamped in bright colours with marble counters. Customers return again and again for excellent fudge-like barfis, sticky jalebi and takeaway packets of rasmalai. Savoury snacks include crisp vegetable samosas and packets of Bombay mix.

Indian Spice Shop
115-119 Drummond Street, NW1
(020-7-916 1831)
Tube: Euston
Open: Mon-Sat 9.30am-9.30pm;
Sun 10am-9pm
Catering for both the local English and Indian communities, this is divided into an off-licence-cum-corner shop on one side and an Indian grocer's on the other which offers an excellent range of spices, chutneys, papads and dals, plus huge sacks of basmati.

EAST

Focal points for Indian shopping in the East End are the area around Brick Lane (home to the Bengali community); and, further out, Green Street in Upton Park.

Ambala
55 Brick Lane, E1
(020-7-247 8569)
Tube: Aldgate East
Open: Mon-Sat 10am-8pm;
Sun 9.30am-7.30pm
A branch of the Asian sweet manufacturers (see under Central for more details).

Taj Stores
112-14a Brick Lane, E1
(020-7-377 0061)
Tube: Aldgate East
Open: Mon-Sun 9am-9pm
A comprehensive food store, serving the local Bengali community, which combines a halal meat counter, a greengrocer's section and a mini-supermarket of grocery items such as pulses and spices.

Green Street, E7
Tube: Upton Park
This long East End road is characterised by a mixture of High Street chain stores, a jellied eel and mash shop and an assortment of Asian stores, selling everything from wedding saris and gold jewellery to bargain boxes of mangoes and sweetmeats.

Bharat
4-6 Carlton Terrace,
Green Street, E7
(020-8-572 6393)
Tube: Upton Park
Open: Mon-Sun 9am-8pm
This large store is aimed at those who buy
in bulk, stocking things like huge 15 litre
tins of ghee and 10 kilogram sacks of
basmati. The freezers are jammed with
Indian fast food, from halal kofta kebabs to
spicy chicken nuggets. Fresh fruit and veg,
such as aubergines and chillies, can be
found at Bharat's small sister shop, over the
road at No. 263.

Green Village
10a Carlton Terrace
Green Street, E7
(020-8-503 4809)
Tube: Upton Park
Open: Daily 8am-7pm
A large, neat greengrocer's, full of the smell
of ripe mangoes at the time of my visit. Stock
included more unusual items such as rolls of
patra leaves, gunda (used in chutneys), sweet
tamarind pods and Thai mangosteens.

Kishan The Mill Shop
20 Carlton Terrace
Green Street, E7
(020-8-471 0008)
Tube: Upton Park
Open: Mon-Sat 9am-7pm; Sun 10am-6pm
A grocers, with a large selection of spices,
cooking oils, nuts, nibbles (such as cassava
chips) and pulses, and brightly-coloured
garlands of flowers hanging down behind
the till.

Queens Market
Green Street, E7 (on the corner of Queen Road)
Tube: Upton Park
Open: Tue & Thur-Sat 8am-5pm
Stalls here sell an assortment of goods, from
curtain fabric to household wares. The
presence of a local Asian community is
reflected in a number of halal butcher's and
fishmonger's selling Asian fish around the
edge of the market.

Sunfresh
11-12 Carlton Terrace
Green Street, E7
(020-8-470 3031)
Tube: Upton Park
Open: Open: Daily 8am-7pm
Funky music blares in this large store which
offers both an array of Indian fruit and veg
and a grocery section with rice, pulses,
chutneys and spices.

NORTH

Goodeats
124 Ballards Lane, N3
(020-7-349 2373)
Tube: Finchley Central
Open: Mon-Sat 9am-7pm
A small, friendly neatly-arranged Asian
foodstore. In addition to a good selection of
Indian groceries, there is a fresh fruit and
vegetable section, including fresh methi,
mangoes and patra.

Q Stores
19 Lodge Lane, N12
(020-8-446 2495)
Tube: Woodside Park
Open: Mon-Sat 9.30am-5.45pm;
Sun 10am-1pm
Tucked away just off North Finchley's busy
high street, this small, neat shop has a good
range of fresh Indian produce, from mangoes
to methi, plus store cupboard staples.

NORTH WEST

For an excellent choice of Indian food
shops, especially greengrocer's, visit
Wembley's Ealing Road. Be warned,
however, that it becomes very busy over the
weekend and parking restrictions have made
it hard to leave the car nearby.

Fudco
184 Ealing Road, HA0
(020-8-902 4820)
Tube: Alperton
Open: Mon-Sat 9.30am-6.30pm;
Sun 10.30am-6.30pm
As importers and packagers, Fudco are a major supplier of foostuffs ranging from spices to dried fruits. Their own grocer's shop, is a showcase for their own brand goods, offering everything from chickpea flour to an assortment of dried chillies.

Obhrai
168–170 Ealing Road, HA0
(020-8-903 4450)
Tube: Alperton
Open: Mon-Sun 9am-7pm
A cash and carry store with a good range of groceries including spices, pulses, flours, pickles and tinned vegetables.

Royal Sweets
280 Ealing Road, HA0
(020-8-903 9359)
Tube: Alperton
Open: Tue-Sun 10am-7pm

A friendly branch of the established Asian sweetmeat shop, selling brightly coloured halvas and savoury nibbles.

Sira Fruit–Veg
288 Ealing Road, HA0
(020-8-903 5769)
Tube: Alperton
Open: Mon-Sun 8am-10pm
A roomy store with a large fresh fruit and vegetable section, including okra, fresh curry leaves and bunches of methi. In addition is a selection of basic Asian groceries.

V. B. & Sons Cash and Carry
218 Ealing Road, HA0
(020-8-902 8579)
Tube: Alperton
Open: Mon-Fri 9.30am-6.45pm;
Sat 9am-6.45pm; Sun 11am-5pm
A huge, neatly-arranged store, aromatic with spices and bustling with customers tracking down the numerous special offers. V.B. specialises in groceries, with a huge range of spices, nuts, dried fruits, dals and flours. The freezer section contains yucca and mogo chips, samosas and samosa pastry.

Drumsticks

ASIAN LONDON

Wembley Exotics
133-135 Ealing Road, HA0
(020-8-900 2607)
Tube: Alperton
Open: Daily 24 hours
Mounds of chillies, root ginger and peanuts under an awning mark this huge cavernous self-service store, which specialises in fresh produce. Inside is a staggering array of Asian fruits and vegetables, from guvar beans and pigeon peas to guavas and mangoes.

Saya Enterprises
Meadow Garth Road, NW10
(020 8 965 8387)
Tube: Neasden
Open: Daily 10am-8pm
Tucked away in the Neasden Hindu temple's car park is this small store, which offers a range of Asian fruits and vegetables, store-cupboard basics and a choice of sweet and savoury nibbles.

SOUTH

Dadu
198–99 Upper Tooting Road, SW17
(020-8-672 4984)
Tube: Tooting Bec or Tooting Broadway
Open: Mon–Sat 9am–7pm; Sun 10am–5pm
A huge Asian supermarket with aisles of spices, chutneys, rice and flours (such as besan and chupatti flour).

Deepak Cash and Carry
953 Garratt Lane, SW17
(020-8-767 7819)
Tube: Tooting Broadway
Open: Mon–Sat 9am–7.30pm; Sun 10am-4pm
An enormous, rather ramshackle supermarket with an extensive range of Asian foodstuffs, from provisions like poppadums and chutneys to fresh fruit and vegetables.

Everfresh Ltd
204-208 Upper Tooting Road, SW17
(020-8-672 7396)
Tube: Tooting Bec or Tooting Broaday
Open: Mon–Sun 7am–7pm
A self-service fruit and vegetable superstore, with everything neatly arranged and most items clearly labelled. Filled with customers carefully choosing their own produce, it has an excellent general selection of Asian goods.

Patel Brothers
187–91 Upper Tooting Road, SW17
(020-8-672 2792)
Tube: Tooting Bec or Tooting Broadway
Open: Mon–Sun 9am–6.30pm
A large store with a fresh fruit and vegetable section near the door. Stock includes shelves of pickles, curry pastes and spices, ghee and tinned foods. A side room is devoted mainly to rice, pulses and flours, including 32 kilogram sacks of chapati flour.

WEST

Southall, in London's outer suburbs, is a busy Indian shopping area full of sari shops, jewellers, halal butchers, greengrocers and large-scale cash and carry stores, where the emphasis is on bulk-buying.

Ambala
107 The Broadway, UB1
(020-8-843 9049)
BR: Southall
Open: Mon–Sun 10am–8pm
A large branch of the established Asian sweet manufacturers.

Dokal & Sons
133–135 The Broadway, UB1
(020-8-574 1647)
BR: Southall
Open: Mon–Sun 9am–8pm
What appears at first to be a small corner shop widens out into a huge store, filled with a comprehensive stock of groceries

such as chutneys, flours, tinned vegetables, nuts and spices. Now in its 25th year, it is run with friendly enthusiasm by Mr Dokal and his family.

Gifto Cash and Carry
115–119 The Broadway, UB1
(020-8-574 8602)
BR: Southall
Open: Mon–Sun 9am–8pm
Well-established and resembling a mini-supermarket, Gifto's is a classic Southall cash and carry. Stock includes basics such as rice and dal, a freezer of frozen seafood such as kingfish steaks, tubs of ghee and a range of spices and condiments.

Sira Cash and Carry
128 The Broadway, UB1
(020-8-574 2280)
BR: Southall
Open: Mon–Sun 8am–8pm
A roomy shop with a good range of stock including flours, pulses, spices and chutneys. In addition there is an excellent, extensive greengrocer's section with an aisle of fruit including chikoo, limes, guavas and tiny green mangoes for pickling and Asian vegetables, such as karela, tindola and fresh chickpeas.
also at: *43 South Road, UB1*
(020-8-571 4529); Open: Mon–Sun 8am–9pm

Mail order

The Curry Club
PO Box 7
Haslemere
Surrey
GU27 1EP

EATING PLACES

CENTRAL

Diwana Bhel Poori House £
121 Drummond Street, NW1
(020-7-387 5566)
Tube: Euston
A well-established, unpretentious South-Indian vegetarian restaurant, deservedly popular for its delicious dosai, idlee and good value thali.

Great Nepalese ££
48 Eversholt Street, NW1
(020-7-388 6737)
Tube: Euston
A Euston institution, much-frequented by hungry commuters, which in addition to standard curry house fare has a selection of Nepalese specialities.

India Club ££
Strand Continental Hotel
143 Strand, WC2
(020-7-836 0650)
Tube: Temple
A long-established restaurant recommended by Indian friends, this is an unpretentious, friendly restaurant which offers good North Indian food at very reasonable prices.

Indian YMCA £
41 Fitzroy Square, W1
(020-7-387 0411)
Tube: Warren Street
The appetising smell of Indian cooking wafts out from this large building, adding character to its institutional air. On offer is good home-style food at student prices in a canteen atmosphere.

Malabar Junction ££
107 Great Russell Street, WC1
(020-7-580 5230)
Tube: Tottenham Court Road
A rather drab frontage hides a large airy restaurant complete with a glass roof. South-Indian cuisine is the speciality here, from tangy iddly (steamed rice and black gram cakes) to spicy Keralan fish curry. Service is courteous and prices very reasonable given the standard of the cooking.

Raavi Kebab Halal Tandoori £
125 Drummond Street, NW1
Tube: Euston Square
(020-7-388 1780)
A small, unpretentious restaurant which specialises in delicious, chilli-hot kebabs, freshly-grilled over charcoal.

Ragam ££
57 Cleveland Street, W1
(020-7-636 9098)
Tube: Goodge Street or Warren Street
A small, modest and friendly restaurant serving excellent, good value food including South-Indian dishes such as avial or uthappam, and delicious breads.

Rasa Samudra ££££
5 Charlotte Street, W1
(020-7-637 0222)
Tube: Goodge Street
This is the latest Rasa restaurant, specialising in Keralan seafood dishes such as kingfish and green mango curry, and crab in coconut milk.

Rasa W1 £££
6 Dering Street, W1
(020-7-629 1346)
Tube: Oxford Circus or Bond Street
One of a new wave of smart Indian restaurants in London offering authentic regional cooking rather than curry-house staples. Keralan vegetarian cuisine is on offer here, giving the chance to try distinctive

spiced dishes such as green banana and mango curry and cashew nut patties. Round off your meal with Keralan desserts such as banana dosa (pancakes) or pal payasum (cashew rice pudding).

Ravi Shankar £
133-135 Drummond Street, NW1
(020-7-388 6458)
Tube: Euston
A smart, popular Indian vegetarian restaurant offering reasonably priced dishes such as masala or de luxe dosai.

Veeraswamy £££
99 Regent Street, W1
(020-7-734 1401)
Tube: Piccadilly Circus
London's oldest Indian restaurant has shed its Raj image. Now owned by the Chutney Mary team it is now a sleek example of new-wave Indian restaurants, complete with vividly painted walls, smartly dressed staff and a menu offering regional dishes.

EAST

Cafe Spice Namaste ££££
16 Prescott Street, E1
(020-7-488 9242)
Tube: Aldgate East or Tower Hill
Chef Cyrus Todiwala is committed to the bringing of true Indian cookery, in all its variety and glory, to the London restaurant scene. From within a brightly-decorated old courthouse he serves up dishes from an extensive menu, including many rarely-found Goan and Parsee dishes.

Lahore Kebab House £
2 Umberstone Street, E1
(020-7-481 9737)
Tube: Whitechapel
One of the best known of the Whitechapel Indian restaurants, still offering bargain-price Pakistani dishes, including excellent kebabs.

NORTH

Bengal Lancer ££
253 Kentish Town Road, NW5
(020-7-485 6688)
Tube: Kentish Town
A lively, popular North Indian restaurant offering good attentive service and curry-house classics at reasonable prices.

Jai Krishna £
161 Stroud Green Road, N4
(020-7-272 1680)
Tube: Finsbury Park
An unpretentious restaurant offering cheap Indian vegetarian food. Refreshingly, the menu includes unusual Indian vegetables such as tindora and dudi curries.

Majjo's £
1 Fortis Green Road, N2
(020-8-883 4357)
Tube: East Finchley
This small, smart, friendly take-away offers superior Pakistani home-cooking produced by Majjo and her assistants, which is enjoyed by a host of regulars. The meat is halal and there is a range of more unusual vegetarian dishes such as patra. Sample tastes are offered to those trying to choose from the array of dishes on offer.

Rani ££
7 Long Lane, N3
(020-8-349 4386/2646)
Tube: Finchley Central
A stylish Gujarati restaurant serving top-notch vegetarian cuisine. All dishes, from the homemade chutneys to the breads, are carefully prepared, and the exciting range includes delights such as banana methi and tindora curry.

ASIAN LONDON

NORTH-WEST

Geeta £
57-59 Willesden Lane, NW6
(020-7-624 1713)
Tube: Kilburn
Specialising in South Indian cuisine, this
cosy restaurant offers authentic dishes at
reasonable prices.

Karahi King £
213 East Lane, HA0
(020-8-904 2760/4994)
Tube: North Wembley
Despite being distinctly off the beaten track,
housed in a non-descript arcade of shops just
off the North Circular, the Karahi King
does excellent business – as the row of cars
parked outside testifies. The decor is
functional, but the service is polite and the
food gutsy and tasty: from grilled kebabs to
Karahi Lamb Chops – tiny, flavourful chops
in a rich, thick tomato-based sauce. It's
unlicensed but you can stock up next with
booze at the off-licence next door.

Sabras £
263 High Road, NW10
(020-8-459 0340)
Tube: Dollis Hill
Highly acclaimed for its subtle and delicious
Gujurati food, this restaurant is a popular
local institution.

Sakonis £
119-121 Ealing Road, HA0
(020-8-903 9601)
Tube: Alperton
A bright, roomy vegetarian restaurant, filled
with families tucking into snacks and dishes
like aloo chat and dosai. There's a wide
choice of drinks and desserts, including
falooda, chikoo ice-cream and delicious,
salty-sweet freshly-squeezed lime juice.

SOUTH

Chutney Mary ££££
535 King's Road, SW10
(020-7-351 3113)
Tube: Fulham Broadway
A pioneering Anglo-Indian restaurant, this
was among the first to offer London diners
the chance to try authentic regional Indian
dishes. Surroundings are grand and the
menu extensive – the Sunday brunch is
particularly popular.

Shree Krishna £
192-194 Tooting High Street, SW17
(020-8-672 4250)
Tube: Tooting Broadway
This large restaurant is full of enthusiasts
who appreciate both the good South Indian
vegetarian food and the reasonable prices.

WEST

Madhu's Brilliant £
39 South Road, UB1
(020-8-574 1897)
BR: Southall
A popular Southall eaterie, attracting Asians
and non-Asians alike, which serves tasty
Punjabi food such as Masala Fish and Karahi
Chicken, with good breads.

Sagoo and Takhar £
114–116 The Green, UB2
(020-8-574 2597)
BR: Southall
A down-to-earth, self-service curry house
where you can eat tasty North Indian food
at very reasonable prices.

COOKBOOKS

Classic Indian Cooking
Julie Sahni
A well-written Indian cookery book which
is readable, useable and authoritative.

Classic Indian Vegetarian Cooking
Julie Sahni
An inspirational book filled with appetising
recipes conveying the less well-known
world of Indian vegetarian cuisine in all its
subtlety.

Flavours of India
Madhur Jaffrey
An attractive regional tour of Indian
cookery containing some unusual recipes.

Madhur Jaffrey's Indian Cookery
A clearly-written, accessible introduction to
the cuisine.

Fifty Great Curries of India
Camellia Panjabi
A beautifully-presented, in-depth illustrated
guide to the art of making curries, from
Bombay Crab Curry to Delhi Butter
Chicken, by the Marketing Director of
India's Taj Hotel group.

ASIAN LONDON

CHINESE LONDON

Phoenix Chinese Food

The original points of entry for the Chinese community in Britain were Liverpool and London: the ports into which Chinese seamen with the East India Company arrived and settled. The Limehouse area, near the docks in the East End, was London's first 'Chinatown', with the first immigrants arriving during the eighteenth century when Britain's tea trade with China was booming. Sailors jumped ship and set up businesses running laundries, shops or becoming ship's chandlers. In the 1950s, the development of the laundromat and the domestic washing machine badly affected the laundry business, so catering became an alternative source of work.

Limehouse was practically destroyed in the Blitz, when the docks were a major target for enemy bombers, and post-war restrictive regulations imposed on non-British workers by the Seamen's Union badly affected Chinese seamen. So, both alternative livelihoods and accommodation had to be found. Soho, a run-down, derelict area with a bad reputation and low property prices, saw an influx of Chinese around the Gerrard Street area in the 1950s. The first Chinese restaurants in Soho were chop-suey outlets, opened in the 1940s to cater for American GIs and British servicemen who had acquired a taste for Chinese food overseas. Restaurants catering specifically for the growing Chinese community also opened in the area. The Communist revolution in China in 1949 meant a further wave of immigration from

China into Britain in the 1950s and 1960s, mostly from the British colony of Hong Kong. As a result, the Chinese community in Soho expanded further.

The area bounded by Shaftesbury Avenue, Leicester Square, Charing Cross Road and Wardour Street is a rectangle of predominantly Chinese shops, businesses, gambling clubs and restaurants. Gerrard Street, now pedestrianized, comes complete with Chinese-style arches and pagoda-style phone boxes.

Two annual festivals have become major events in London, attracting people from outside the Chinese community. Chinese New Year, according to the Chinese lunar calendar, takes place either in late January or early February, and is celebrated with gifts to children of 'ang pow', money in lucky red envelopes, and a lion dance procession. Special dishes appear on menus in the restaurants. Each year is attributed to one of the twelve animals in the Chinese zodiac – with the year of the dragon being especially auspicious – and the New Year celebrations feature the animal to which the year belongs. The autumnal Moon Festival, around September, is marked by special moon cakes and a lion dance. During both these festivals, Chinatown is filled with Chinese of all generations, colourful lanterns and decorations and street stalls selling snacks and gifts.

CHINESE CUISINE

This ancient cuisine is both complex and various. Underlying it are the 'yin and yang' principles, translated in culinary terms into hot, cold and neutral, with ingredients allocated different properties. A huge range of ingredients is used, with nothing wasted. There is an old saying that 'A Cantonese will eat anything with four legs except for a piece of furniture and anything that flies apart from a kite'. Textures play an important role in Chinese cooking and include some that are foreign to Western sensibilities, with slippery, jelly-like textures being prized.

Each of China's regions has its own characteristic cuisine, influenced by climate and the availability of ingredients. It's customary, however, to group China culinarily into four broad geographical groups: Peking/Northern, Shanghai/Eastern, Szechuan/Western and Cantonese/Southern. The cuisine of the North is distinguished by its use of grains other than rice, such as wheat, corn and millet, in the form of breads, noodles, dumplings and pancakes. Because the ancient Imperial Court was situated in Peking, elaborate dishes such as Peking Duck are characteristic of this cuisine. The Mongols introduced lamb, which is eaten more widely here than in other parts of China.

Eastern cuisine is famous for its fresh fish and seafood. Rich, sweet seasonings are a hallmark and popular techniques include stir-frying, steaming, red-cooking (slow simmering in soy sauce) and blanching. Szechuan cooking, from the provinces of Hunan, Yunnan and Szechuan in Western China, is marked by its use of fiery chillies, garlic, ginger and Szechuan peppercorns producing a vigorous, strongly flavoured cuisine. Two regional foodstuffs are the aromatic peppercorns and chilli-pickled mustard plant.

Cantonese cuisine is the best-known Chinese cooking outside China, because of the large numbers of Chinese from southern Canton who emigrated in the nineteenth century. Strong, overwhelming flavourings are avoided and, instead, a harmonious blend of colours, textures and flavours is sought. Stir-frying epitomises Cantonese cooking, with the freshness and colours of ingredients retained and a minimum of seasonings added. Dimsum, the small steamed and fried dumplings eaten at lunchtime, are another Cantonese speciality.

GLOSSARY

Agar agar: a vegetarian setting agent obtained from seaweed which does not require refrigeration to set. Available either in powdered form or translucent strands.

Azuki beans: small red beans, used primarily in cakes and desserts and available both whole and in sweetened paste form.

Bamboo shoots: fresh bamboo shoots are occasionally available. Tinned bamboo shoots, either whole or sliced, are easily found.

Bean curd (doufu): a soy bean product which has always been a valuable source of protein in Chinese cooking. Fresh ivory-coloured bean curd has a firm custard texture and bland flavour. It is sold in the chilled section, packed in water. Deep-fried bean curd has a golden colour and spongy texture and is found in packets in the chilled section. Bean curd 'cheese', either red or white, is fermented bean curd with a strong, salty taste and is sold in jars. Dried bean-curd sheets are sold in packets.

Bean sprouts: white crispy sprouts of the mung bean; also available are the larger, nuttier soya bean sprouts, which should be cooked before eating.

Beche-de-mer: sea cucumber or sea slug, sold dried and prized as a delicacy.

Bird's nest: the key ingredient of the famous delicacy, bird's nest soup. The nests of a species of cave-dwelling swallow are coated with a gelatinous saliva and it is this which gives the soup its prized consistency. The nests are sold either whole or in fragments for high prices.

Black beans: small black soya beans, fermented with salt and spices, with a pungent flavour.

Chilli oil: a transparent oil, tinted red from chillies, sold in small bottles and with a powerful chilli kick.

Chinese broccoli (gaai laan): a thick-stalked vegetable with large rounded leaves and white flowers.

Ginger

48

Chinese cabbage (bok choy): similar in appearance to Swiss chard, with dark green leaves and thick white stems. Green bok choy, with green leaves and stems, is also available.

Chinese chives: long, dark green, flat leaves, with a stronger and more pungent odour and flavour than English chives; also sold blanched and complete with buds.

Chinese cinnamon: cassia bark, sold in sticks similar to cinnamon but larger and rougher with a stronger flavour.

Chinese flowering cabbage (choi sum): a leafy vegetable with rounded leaves, small yellow flowers and long stems.

Chinese leaves: a large tight head of white-green crinkly leaves with a crunchy texture; widely available.

Chinese mushrooms: black, dried shitake mushrooms with a distinctive meaty flavour. Prices vary according to the size and thickness of the caps.

Chinese sausages: these resemble small, fatty salamis, but they must be cooked before eating. There are two sorts: pork and pork and liver, the latter being darker in colour. They are found in packets or hanging up in bunches with other dried meats.

Coriander: this green herb, similar in appearance to flat-leaved continental parsley but with a distinctive sharp flavour, is one of the few herbs used in Chinese cooking.

Five-spice powder: fragrant, golden-brown powder made from five or sometimes six ground spices, with the four base spices being star-anise, Chinese cinnamon, cloves and fennel seeds. Szechuan peppercorns, ginger and cardamom are the additions.

Ginger: an aromatic root available fresh.

Glutinous rice: rounded rice grains with a sticky texture when cooked, used in both sweet and savoury dishes.

Golden needles: long dried buds of the tiger-lily flower.

Longan: a small brown-skinned fruit, related to the lychee, with translucent flesh and glossy black seed (also known as 'dragon's eye' fruit). Available either tinned or fresh.

Lotus leaves: the large leaves of the water-lily plant, available dried and used to wrap food for cooking.

Lotus root: a crunchy root with a decorative tracery of holes, available fresh, in sausage-like links, or tinned.

Mooli: a large, long white radish, with crispy white flesh.

Mustard Greens (gaai choi): a green large-leafed plant. The bitter varieties are pickled rather than cooked.

Noodles: cellophane noodles (also known as beanthread, glass or transparent noodles): fine thread-like noodles made from mung beans and need soaking before they can be easily cut; egg noodles: made from wheat flour, egg and water, distinguished by their yellow colour; rice noodles and vermicelli are dried, white noodles of varying widths made from rice flour which need soaking before use; river rice noodles (sarhor noodles) are made from ground rice and water, steamed in thin sheets and cut into strips. Fresh-river rice noodles are sold in clear packets, and usually stored near the chilled section.

CHINESE LONDON

49

Potato flour: fine white flour, made from cooked potatoes, used as a thickener.

Rice vinegar: mild vinegars, ranging from delicate white rice vinegar to sweet red rice vinegar and rich black rice vinegar.

Rice wine: made from glutinous rice, yeast and water, this is used for both drinking and cooking.

Sauces: chilli bean sauce: a hot, spicy, dark sauce made from soya beans and chillies; chilli sauce, a bright red sweet chilli sauce; hoisin sauce, a thick, brown fruity sauce; oyster sauce, a thick, brown sauce made from oysters; soy sauce, a dark brown salty liquid made from fermented soya beans (available as thin, salty Light Soy Sauce or as thicker, sweeter Dark Soy Sauce); and yellow bean sauce: a thick, brown sauce made from fermented yellow beans.

Sesame oil: a nutty, golden-coloured oil made from sesame seeds.

Shrimps, dried: small, shelled, dried pink shrimps, with a strong salty flavour.

Spring roll wrappers: white paper-thin wrappers, available in different sizes. Found in either the chilled or freezer sections.

Star-anise: dark brown, star-shaped pod with a distinctive licorice flavour and scent.

Straw mushrooms: cone-shaped mushrooms, usually available canned.

Szechuan peppercorns: fragrant, reddish-brown 'peppercorns', which are the dried berries of a shrub.

Szechuan pickled vegetables: mustard green roots, pickled in salt and hot chillies, which are a speciality of Szechuan province.

Tangerine peel: in its dried form, in dark-brown pieces, this is used as a flavouring in Chinese cooking.

Thousand-year-old eggs: preserved duck eggs, with a pungent flavour, which are in fact only about a hundred days old.

Water chestnuts: the crunchy bulbs of a waterplant. Fresh, brown-skinned bulbs are sometimes found, but tinned water chestnuts are easily available.

Water spinach (ong chai): a triangular-leafed plant with a mild, spinach-like flavour.

Winter melon: a large green gourd with white flesh, available whole or in pieces, and often used to make soup.

Wonton skins: small squares of yellow egg-noodle dough, used to wrap up dumplings. Found in either chilled or freezer sections.

Wood ears: black, crinkled, dried fungus with a beige underside.

FOODSHOPS

B asic Chinese flavourings such as root ginger or soy sauce are easily available, but for the more unusual ingredients and especially the large range of fresh Chinese vegetables, the Gerrard Street area remains the best for Chinese food shopping. Although prices for the vegetables may seem high, they are normally of excellent quality and freshness, having been sorted before packing. There is, however, the disconcerting habit in many Chinese shops of offering both fruit and vegetables in pre-packed quantities, often as large as 2lbs in weight.

CENTRAL

Far East
13 Gerrard Street, W1
(020-7-437 6148)
Tube: Leicester Square
Open: Mon-Sun 10am-7pm
A friendly bakery and tea shop selling Chinese cakes and pastries including sticky, glazed char-siu buns, curry beef puffs and egg custard tarts.

Golden Gate Grocers
16 Newport Place, WC2
(020-7-437 6266)
Tube: Leicester Square
Open: Mon-Sun 10am-7.45pm
A small but well-stocked foodshop with a good range of Chinese vegetables displayed outside: boxes of bok choy, gaai laan, mooli, piles of durians, boxes of Thai mangoes and mangosteens – helpfully labelled in English.

Golden Gate Hong Supermarket
14 Lisle Street, WC2
(020-7-437 0014)
Tube: Leicester Square
Open: Mon-Sun 9am-8.30pm
Boxes of fresh fruit and vegetables under a canopy signal this pleasant, neatly-arranged shop. The vegetables inside are labelled in English and there is good basic stock.

Good Harvest Fish and Meat Market
14 Newport Place, WC2
(020-7-437 0712)
Tube: Leicester Square
Open: Mon-Sun 11am-7pm
Chinatown's only fishmonger offers fresh scallops in their shells, live lobsters, raw king prawns and more unusual fish including catfish, seabass and pomfret.

Loon Fung Supermarket
42-44 Gerrard Street, W1
(020-7-437 7332)
Tube: Leicester Square
Open: Mon-Sun 10am-8pm
Around thirty years old, Loon Fung is the oldest and largest Chinese supermarket in Soho, occupying a key slot on Gerrard Street and always bustling with customers. Boxes of fresh fruit such as lychees, longans and persimmons, are displayed outside on the pavement with a large fresh vegetable section inside. A butcher's counter sells basic cuts plus more unusual items such as duck and chicken feet and ducks' tongues. All the staples are stocked across a wide range.

Loon Moon Supermarket
9a Gerrard Street, W1
(020-7-734 9940)
Tube: Leicester Square
Open: Mon-Sun 10.30am-8pm
This old-fashioned shop has a small fresh vegetable section, including Thai produce such as pea aubergines and Thai basils, but is strong on tinned and bottled foods. There is a large back room with chilled and freezer sections and a good choice of spices.

CHINESE LONDON

51

Newport Supermarket

28-29 Newport Court, WC2
(020-7-437 2386)
Tube: Leicester Square
Open: Mon-Sun 10.30am-8pm
This corner supermarket has an excellent selection of Chinese vegetables and fruit on display outside. Inside, the roomy shop, complete with freezer and chilled sections, contains a good choice of ingredients.

Phoenix Chinese Food

39 Wardour Street, W1
(020-7-437 1956)
Tube: Leicester Square
Open: Mon-Sun 11am-8pm
This take-away restaurant specialises in pre-cooked meats such as red char siu or barbecued pork, soya chicken and roast duck. The window is a carnivore's delight: a cooked pig, split in two, dangles among strings of roast ducks and piles of intestines.

See Woo

19 Lisle Street, WC2
(020-7-439 8325)
Tube: Leicester Square
Open: Mon-Sun 10am-8pm
This large, sprawling shop has an excellent, comprehensive stock: chilled, frozen, dried, tinned and bottled. There is a large fresh fruit and vegetable section, which regularly has more unusual items. A basement room contains bowls of all sizes, woks, steamers and other Chinese cookware.

NORTH

Maysun Markets

869 Finchley Road, NW11
(020-8-455 4773)
Tube: Golders Green
Open: Mon-Sat 9am-7.30pm
A small, crowded shop selling a mixture of household goods and Chinese foodstuffs. It has a basic stock of dried, bottled and tinned ingredients and a few fresh basics.

Wing Yip (London) Ltd

395 Edgware Road, NW2
(020-8-450 0422)
Tube: Colindale
Open: Mon-Sat 9.30am-7pm;
Sun 11.30am-5.30pm
This enormous superstore at Staples Corner is the place for bulk-buying Chinese food. It has an impressive selection, ranging from freezers of dim sum to delicacies such as bird's nest and shark's fin. There is a small selection of fresh vegetables and foodstuffs such as beancurd and noodles.

SOUTH

Wing Thai Supermarket

13, Electric Avenue, SW9
(020-7-738 5898)
Tube: Brixton
Open: Mon-Sat 10am-7pm
Hidden behind the bustling fruit and veg stalls outside, this roomy store has a small fresh produce section, but is particularly strong on bottled, tinned and frozen goods.

Loon Fung Supermarket

EATING PLACES

L ondon's Chinese restaurants offer predominantly Cantonese food. As such, several places offer excellent dimsum – an assortment of steamed and fried dumplings served at lunchtime – which are a speciality of Canton.
With Chinatown overrun by tourists, standards have slipped in many of its restaurants, though some continue to offer excellent meals. If you enjoy good Chinese food, then you could also head for Bayswater, where a cluster of excellent Chinese restaurants attract enthusiastic and discerning diners.

CENTRAL

China China £££
3 Gerrard Street, W1
(020-7-439 7511)
Tube: Leicester Square
A busy, efficient restaurant offering straight-forward down-to-earth Cantonese food.

China City £££
White Bear Yard
25a Lisle Street, WC2
(020-7-734 3388)
Tube: Leicester Square
Tucked away in a courtyard off a Soho side street, this roomy restaurant offers good dimsum and an extensive Cantonese menu.

Fung Shing £££
15 Lisle Street, WC2
(020-7-437 1539)
Tube: Leicester Square
A peaceful, civilized restaurant noted for its authentic food, offering impeccable versions of dishes such as black bean braised hotpot and duck and plum sauce hotpot.

Golden Dragon £££
28-29 Gerrard Street, W1
(020-7-734 2763)
Tube: Leicester Square
Large, gaudily-decorated with splendid writhing dragons and efficiently staffed, this is a quintessential Chinatown restaurant. It's noted for its dimsum and is correspondingly busy at lunchtime on a Sunday.

Jen £££
7 Gerrard Street, W1
(020-7-287 8193)
Tube: Leicester Square
Distinctly dapper with polite staff, the menu offers the chance to try more unusual dishes, such as yam-stuffed spring rolls.

New World £££
1 Gerrard Place, W1
(020-7-434 0396)
Tube: Leicester Square
Vast and bright, New World offers straightforward Cantonese food and dimsum, served from trolleys.

Poons £££
4 Leicester Street, WC2
(020-7-437 1528)
Tube: Leicester Square
A veteran Chinatown name, tucked away in a side street, this restaurant continues to offer reasonably-priced, flavourful Cantonese food including speciality wind-dried meats.

EAST

Old Friend £££
659 Commercial Road, E14
(020-7-790 5027)
DLR: Limehouse
Claiming to be London's oldest Chinese restaurant, this Cantonese eaterie is a remnant from the days when the city's Chinese community was concentrated around the Limehouse area.

Shanghai £££
41 Kingsland High Street, E8
(020-7-254 2878)
BR: Dalston Kingsland
What was formerly an original eel and pie shop has now been transformed into a busy Chinese restaurant. Good dimsum and a bargain lunchtime buffet pull in the punters.

NORTH

Cheng Du £££
9 Parkway, NW1
(020-7-485 8058)
Tube: Camden Town
A tastefully smart restaurant, offering elegantly-served Sezchuan classics such as double-cooked pork.

Green Cottage ££
9 New College Parade
Finchley Road, NW3
(020-7-722 5305)
Tube: Finchley Road
A down-to-earth restaurant offering Chinatown-standard Cantonese food in a North London setting.

Vegetarian Cottage ££
91 Haverstock Hill, NW3
(020-7-586 1257)
Tube: Belsize Park
An attractive restaurant offering traditional Chinese Buddhist vegetarian dishes, including many that mimic meat in texture. Service is pleasant and the food, including several bean curd dishes, flavourful.

WEST

Hung Toa ££
51 Queensway, W2
(020-7-727 5753)
Tube: Bayswater or Queensway
A small, down-to-earth affair offering excellent one-plate meals, from noodles in soup to congee (savoury rice porridge).

Mandarin Kitchen £££
14-16 Queensway, W2
(020-7-727 9468)
Tube: Bayswater or Queensway
Peering in through the large windows to the dimly-lit interior, one is reminded of an aquarium. Appropriately so, as this large, busy restaurant specialises in Cantonese seafood such as succulent steamed scallops in the shell, and fresh crab with ginger.

Royal China ££
13 Queensway, W2
(020-7-221 2535)
Tube: Bayswater or Queensway
Such is the fame of the dimsum here, that at the weekend, queues start forming before the restaurant opens its doors at noon. Inside, the large, roomy restaurant is decorated with 70s opulence: shiny black tiled walls festooned with golden lacquerwork and masses of mirrors. Service is efficient, which is just as well considering how busy it gets. Dimsum dishes are spot on: from delicate mangetout dumplings (filled with pea-shoots) to spongy char siu bau.
Also at: *40 Baker Street, W1.*

COOKBOOKS

Chinese Cookery
Ken Hom
An accessible, basic introduction to Chinese cooking.

Classic Chinese Cookbook
Yan-Kit So
A truly classic Chinese cookbook, well-illustrated with mouthwatering, workable recipes.

CHINESE LONDON

FRENCH LONDON

Villandry

L ondon's first serious experience of the French was when it fell under Norman rule following the 1066 Conquest. French became the language both of the Court and local government. London saw an influx of merchant traders from northern France and a number of religious orders, including the influential Knights Templar, established themselves in the city.

The next major increase in London's French community was due to the arrival of French-speaking Protestants, known in France as 'Huguenots', who came to England to escape Catholic persecution. In France, the limited privileges granted to Huguenots by the 1598 Edict of Nantes were gradually eroded, with restrictions placed on Protestant worship. In 1680 many Huguenots fled, and Charles II offered them asylum in 1681. Four years later in France, the Edict of Nantes was revoked and Protestant churches were ordered to be destroyed. Following this, between 40,000 and 50,000 Huguenots moved to England, with half of them thought to have settled in London. By the year 1700, Huguenots formed around five per cent of London's population.

Spitalfields and Soho were the two main areas in London in which the Huguenots settled. Spitalfields (also home to a community of Flemish weavers), attracted the Huguenot weavers, who eventually contributed to a prosperous period in the British silk industry. In Soho, where the Huguenots took over a chapel built for Greek Christians and used it until 1822, the new immigrants were craftspeople, such as watch and clockmakers, bookbinders and gold and silversmiths.

Our popular perception of the French as stylish and fashionable was noticeable even then, with a 1700 report declaring, 'The English have now so great an esteem for the workmanship of the French refugees that hardly any thing vends without a gallic name'. Huguenot merchants, alongside other immigrants, played an important part in London's financial life. When the Bank of England was founded in 1694, a number of the founder directors were Huguenots. In addition to influencing crafts and business, Huguenot academics played a notable role in the worlds of science and technology, with many joining the Royal Society.

London's French community also received subsequent groups of refugees, with an influx of royalists fleeing the 1789 French Revolution, and political refugees escaping the 1870 Commune. Gradually, further institutions catering to French expats were set up, from a chapel in the French Embassy to French schools in Lisle Street in 1865. In 1867, the French Hospital and Dispensary in Shaftesbury Avenue was established, while 1893 saw the completion of the French Protestant Church in Soho Square. Paul Villars wrote in 1905 in *Living London* of the French community that 'In London, as in France, they use the café as a club' – the Café Royal was a favourite haunt. During the eighteenth and nineteenth centuries, however, the French community slowly became assimilated into English society. Huguenot families such as the Courthaulds and Oliviers became established members of British society. Today, Spitalfields' Georgian houses and Huguenot names like Fournier Street are reminders of the area's former prosperity under the silk merchants.

During the Second World War, Soho, once home to the Huguenots, was a focal point for the French Resistance, with the York Minster pub acting as the headquarters of the Free French Forces. Generally known 'the French pub' it has now been renamed the French House; General de Gaulle used to shop for his coffee at Angelucci's around the corner on Frith Street.

Today, London's French enclave is in elegant, affluent South Kensington, with the French Lycée on Cromwell Road and the French Institute at Queensberry Place providing two focal points. Serving this community are a cluster of upmarket food shops, including butchers selling French cuts of meat and chic patisseries offering decent croissants and delectable cakes.

FRENCH CUISINE

F rench cuisine has been highly influential throughout Europe, with Britain especially living in its shadow. As the current edition of the Larousse Gastronomique baldly states, 'At the beginning of the twentieth century, French cookery gained supremacy throughout the world.' Today the language of the kitchen continues to be French, from 'chef' to culinary terms such as 'sauté'.

Still a predominantly agricultural country, France has retained many of the regional ingredients such as cheeses, hams or herbs which give its cuisine character and flavour; local markets still abound with locally-grown seasonal produce. Standards of produce have remained high and the simple pleasures of life, such as a decent loaf of bread and some good cheese, are easily found.

An enduring regionalism means that even as we approach the twenty-first century local dishes are cherished, rather than discarded in a mass move towards uniformity. As a result, French cuisine contains wonderfully contrasting strands: from the Mediterranean flavours of Provençal cooking, laden with tomatoes, basil and olive oil; to the dishes of Normandy, flavoured with cider and calvados and rich with the area's famous dairy products.

French cooking can be divided broadly into 'haute cuisine', the cookery of grand restaurants and hotels; 'cuisine du terroir', regional cooking found in provincial restaurants; and 'cuisine grand mere', the everyday food found in people's homes and in cheap, down-to-earth bistros. Haute cuisine has influenced chefs and cookery schools around the world. Naturally, it has followed trends and fashions. In the 1970s and 1980s 'nouvelle cuisine' – a move away from the over-rich dishes of the classic cuisine – was highly influential, although reviled in some quarters for its affectation. In contrast, regional and home cooking continues to stick to a traditional repertoire of classic French dishes, from cassoulet to tarte tatin.

GLOSSARY

Anchovy (anchois): a small seafish, generally available salted in cans or jars, filleted or whole. Its strong flavour plays a key part in dishes like tapenade and pissaladiere.

Bayonne ham: a famous salt-cured, smoked ham, originally from Bayonne but now manufactured all over France.

Butter: pale, unsalted 'sweet' butter from Normandy is highly prized in French pastry-cooking.

Calvados: a spirit distilled from cider traditionally from Normandy. Pays d'Auge Calvados is a particularly high-quality brand.

Capers: the unopened buds of a Mediterranean shrub, used pickled either in brine or vinegar as a distinctive sour flavouring.

Celeriac (céleri-rave): the white, firm-textured, bulbous root of a variety of celery with a distinctive nutty flavour.

Cep (cèpe): a brown-capped, thick-stemmed edible wild boletus mushroom, valued for its rich flavour and meaty texture.

Cheeses: Beaufort, a Gruyère-like hard cow's milk cheese from the mountain pastures of the Savoie; Brie: a circular, soft, unpressed cow's milk cheese, with its origins in the 1200s; Brie de Meaux is a classic brie, farm-made from unpasturised milk; Camembert: a round, flat, soft cheese, traditionally from Normandy; chèvre, goat's milk cheese (mi-chèvre means cheeses made with a mixture of goat's and cow's milks); comte, a Gruyère-type cow's milk cheese from the Jura mountains; crottin de chavignol: a soft goat's milk cheese made in Sancerre, shaped like a small flattened ball; explorateur: a mild, cylindrical, triple-cream cow's milk cheese; Fourme d'Ambert: a semi-soft, cow's milk veined cheese; fromage frais: fresh curd cheese made from cow's milk, used in cooking; livarot, a soft Normandy cow's milk cheese; lucullus: a soft, cylindrical cow's milk cheese; munster, a soft cheese from the Alsace with an orange-red rind; pont l'Eveque: a square-shaped, soft cow's milk cheese from Normandy; and Roquefort: a famous veined, semi-soft sheep's milk cheese, ripened for three months in the limestone caves of Les Causses.

Chervil: a subtley-flavoured green herb, with fine fronds, resembling a delicate continental parsley.

Crème fraîche: soured cream containing a minimum of 30 per cent butterfat.

Dandelion (dent-de-lion, pissenlit): a jagged-leafed, wild meadow plant, dismissed as a weed in England but eaten when young as a salad leaf in France.

Lard de poitrine: a fatty version of streaky bacon used for flavouring dishes such as stews; also available smoked.

Marrons glacés: sweet, glazed, syrup-poached chestnuts, eaten as a costly sweetmeat and used in desserts. Available whole, in pieces or in purée form.

Mustard (moutarde): pale yellow Dijon mustard made from black or brown mustard seeds, verjuice and white wine; mild, aromatic dark-brown Bordeaux mustard; and grainy-textured Meaux mustard made from mixed mustard seeds.

Olive oil: Although a small producer, France's olive oil is well-regarded, with the best thought to come from Provençe.

FRENCH LONDON

59

Pâtés: pâté de campagne, coarse-textured pâté; pâté de foie, containing 15 per cent pork liver and 45 per cent fat.

Purslane (pourpier): a green salad vegetable with rounded, clover-shaped leaves.

Puy lentil: a prized small, green-brown lentil which retains its shape and has a good flavour when cooked.

Rocket (roquette): a peppery, jagged green salad leaf; a traditional element of Provencal mesclun (a wild leaf salad).

Salt cod (morue): dried, salted cod which needs pre-soaking before cooking and is used in classic dishes such as brandade.

Saucisson sec: Dried sausages including: Jésus: a large, pork sausage; saucisson d'Arles, made from pork and beef; saucisson de campagne: made with pork, fat, garlic and spice; rosette, a slowly-matured pure pork sausage.

Sausages: andouillette: a thick, bumpy sausage, sometimes smoked; boudin blanc: a creamy white sausage containing meat such as veal, chicken or pork; boudin noir, a dark-skinned blood sausage made from pig's blood; cervelas: a short, stocky pork sausage; merguez, a spicy red-coloured Algerian lamb and beef sausage; Toulouse: a popular pork cooking sausage, used in cassoulet.

Shallot: a small, russet-skinned, mild member of the onion family.

Snails (escargot): an edible gastropod mollusc, enjoyed by the Gauls, available canned or frozen and sometimes found fresh.

Sorrel: a green, leafy herb with a distinctive sour flavour, used to flavour soups, omelettes and salads.

Tarragon: a fine-leafed green herb with a distinctively, aromatic, faintly aniseed flavour.

Truffle (truffe): rare and costly black and white tubers, with a distinctive aroma and flavour. Black Perigord truffles are particularly prized.

Vanilla sugar: vanilla-flavoured caster sugar, available commercially but easily made at home by placing two or three vanilla pods in a jar of caster sugar and leaving it to infuse.

Wine vinegar: red and white wine vinegars are key flavourings in French cookery, essential in salad dressings. Orleans wine vinegars are particularly valued.

FOODSHOPS

A s one would expect from a country famous for its baking, several of London's distinctly French food shops are elegant patisseries – offering Londoners an all too rare and welcome chance to enjoy decent croissants, delectable cakes and proper bread.

CENTRAL

Bagatelle Boutique
44 Harrington Road, SW7
(020-7-581 1551)
Tube: South Kensington
Open: Mon-Sat 8am-8pm; Sun 8am-6pm
Immaculately elegant, with tempting counter displays and helpful, courteous staff, this large shop sells its own high-quality viennoiserie, patisserie, breads and cakes (all made with Normandy butter and French flour). In addition, there is a traiteur counter offering dishes such as salmon quenelles and homemade foie gras. Finally, to round off, there is a counter of fine French chocolates.

Fileric
57 Old Brompton Road, SW7
(020-7-584 2967)
Tube: South Kensington
Open: Mon-Sat 8am-7pm; Sun 9am-7pm
This tiny, dainty patisserie and salon de thé, much-frequented by the local French community, sells a small but select range of viennoiserie, patisserie and cakes.

The House of Albert Roux
229 Ebury Street, SW1
(020-7-730 4175)
Tube: Sloane Square
Open: Mon-Fri 7.30am-7.30pm;
Sat 7.30-6pm
This chic shop, with an affluent clientele, specialises in French fine foods and traiteur dishes. The latter are made in-house and include Gallic classics such as cassoulet and duck-leg confit. Patisserie products include viennoiserie, elegant cakes and tarts, while mousses and crème brûlée are made to order.

Madeleine
5 Vigo Street, W1
(020-7-734 8353)
Tube: Piccadilly Circus
Open: Mon-Sat 8am-10pm; Sun 11am-7pm
A smart, roomy patisserie-cum-café with a tempting window display of French pastries and cakes such as tarte bonne femme, tarte tatin and religiouse, all freshly-made on the premises.

Maison Bertaux
28 Greek Street, W1
(020-7-437 6007)
Tube: Leicester Square
Open: Mon-Sat 9am-8pm;
Sun 9am-1pm & 3pm-7pm
Established for well over a hundred years, this small patisserie is the last food shop link to Soho's nineteenth-century French community. Tucked away in a backstreet, it has a loyal clientele who enjoy the excellent pastries, good coffee and Bohemian atmosphere, lovingly-sustained by Michelle, the manager. As one sits sipping coffee, trays of freshly-made croissants or fruit tarts are brought out from the kitchen and regulars pause at the till for a few moment's gossip.

Maison Blanc
11 Elystan Street, SW3
(020-7-584 6913)
Tube: South Kensington
Open: Mon-Fri 8.30am-5.30pm;
Sat 8.30am-4.30pm; Sun 8.30am-3.30pm
A branch of the elegant patisserie (see under West for more details).

FRENCH LONDON

Du Pain Duvin

31 Paddington Street, W1
(020-7-224 1758)
Tube: Baker Street
Open: Mon-Fri 10am-8pm; Sat 10am-5pm
This small, pretty tiled food shop (formerly
Wholefood Butcher's) offers a tempting
range of edibles, reflecting owner Eric
Duvin's interest in good food. Bestsellers
here include the range of French chees
(from Brie de Meaux to chèvre) and the
baked quiches and fruit tarts, made on the
premises with French flour, butter, sugar
and cream.

Patisserie Valerie

44 Old Compton Street, W1
(020-7-437 3466)
Tube: Leicester Square
Open: Mon-Fri 8am-8pm;
Sat 8am-7pm; Sun 9.30am-6pm
Very much a Soho institution, this small
patisserie is seemingly always busy serving a
chattering mix of media types. Popular
items include croissants, huge doughnuts
filled with creme patissier and attractive fruit
tarts – perfect for a dinner party dessert.

South Kensington Butchers

19 Bute Street, SW7
(020-7-581 0210)
Tube: South Kensington
Open: Mon-Fri 7.30am-6pm;
Sat 7.30am-5pm
This small, smart-looking butchers caters for
the local French community and sells
French cuts of meat, including roti de veau,
tornados, veau farci and cari d'agneau. In
addition, it stocks white and black boudin,
homemade merguez sausages, goose fat,
bacon lardons and some Fauchon products.

Villandry

170 Great Portland Street, W1
(020-7-631 3131)
Tube: Great Portland Street
Open: Mon-Sat 8.30am-10pm;
Sun 11am-4pm
This swish deli-cum-eaterie has a strong
Gallic element to its upmarket stock.
Highlights are the excellent range of French
farmhouse cheeses and huge assortment of
French dairy products including tangy
Provençal yogurt. In addition there are
Legrand wines, La Maison du Miel honeys
and French ham on the bone. Fresh
produce is also brought in weekly from
France, ranging from summer salad leaves to
wild fungi in the autumn.

NORTH

La Fromagerie

30 Highbury Park, N5
(020-7-359 7440)
Tube: Highbury & Islington
Open: Mon 11am-7.30pm;
Tue-Sat 9.30am-7.30pm; Sun 10am-4.30pm
Under a dark blue awning, a window filled
with appetising tarts and pastries marks the
presence of this attractive shop. As the name
suggests, cheese is the shop's forté and it
stocks between 150–200 farmhouse cheeses
in its cool backroom, of which around 60
per cent are French. Owner Patricia
Michelson makes a point of sourcing
cheeses herself, direct from small farms and
suppliers. The front room is crammed with
edible goodies ranging from dark Black
Cherry jam from the South-West of France
to jars of cassoulet. "Customers can browse
and look and see what we've got and ask us
any questions," says Patricia, whose
enthusiasm for cheese is both genuine and
infectious.

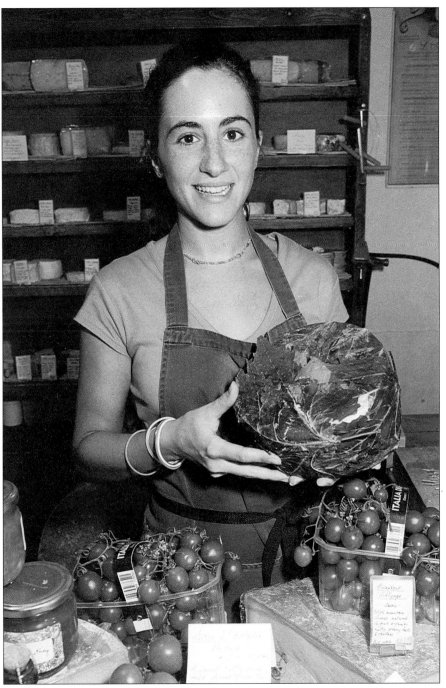

La Fromagerie

Maison Blanc
62 Hampstead High Street, NW3
(020-7-431 8338)
Tube: Hampstead
Open: Mon & Tue 8am-6.30pm; Wed-Sat
8am-7pm; Sun 9am-7pm
A branch of the elegant patisserie (see under
North-West for more details).

NORTH-WEST

Maison Blanc
St John's Wood High Street, NW6
(020-7-586 1982)
Tube: St John's Wood
Open: Mon-Sat 8am-6.30pm; Sun 9am-6pm
An eye-catching display of the most elegant
cakes draws customers into this attractive
French patissierie-cum-salon de thé.
Stock ranges from stoneoven-baked rustic
French breads to cakes such as Concerto, a
melt-in-the-mouth chocolate mousse.
Buches de Noel (at Christmas) and Tarte
Bonne Femme are among the traditional
French goodies on offer.

SOUTH-WEST

Fileric Delicatessen
12 Queenstown Road, SW8
(020-7-720 4844)
Tube: Clapham Common
Open: Mon-Sat 8am-8pm; Sun 8am-4pm
A pleasantly old-fashioned, shop-cum-café
with a delicatessen section offering a range of
French cheeses, sausages, salamis and pâtés.
The pastry counter offers classic French
pastries and cakes, such as tarte citron.

Maison Blanc
303 Fulham Road, SW10
Tube: Gloucester Road
Open: Mon-Sat 8.30am-7pm; Sun 9am-5pm
A branch of the elegant French patisserie
(see under North-West London for more
details)

Maison Blanc
27b The Quadrant, TW9
(020-8-332 7041)
Tube: Richmond
Open: Mon-Wed & Sat 8am-7pm; Thur & Fri
8am-7.30pm; Sun 9am-6pm
A branch of the elegant patisserie (see under
North-West for more details).

WEST

Maison Blanc
102 Holland Park, W11
(020-7-221 2494)
Tube: Holland Park
Open: Mon-Wed 8am-7pm;
Thur & Fri 8am-7.30pm,
Sat 7.30am-7pm; Sun 8.30am-6pm
A branch of the elegant patisserie (see under
North-West for more details).

Maison Blanc
26-28 Turnham Green Terrace, W4
(020-8-995 7220)
Tube: Turnham Green
Open: Mon-Tue 8am-6.30pm;
Wed-Sat 8am-7pm; Sun 9am-6pm
A branch of the elegant patisserie (see under
North-West for more details)

Pierre Pechon
127 Queensway W2
(020-7-229 0746)
Tube: Bayswater or Queensway
Open: Mon-Wed 7am-7pm;
Thur-Sat 7am-8pm; Sun 7.30am-7pm
Since 1925, Pierre Pechon have been selling
a large range of French breads, cakes and
viennoisserie.
Also at: *27 Kensington Church Street, W8*
(020-7-937 9574)

EATING PLACES

CENTRAL LONDON

Madeleine *£*
5 Vigo Street, W1
(020-7-734 8353)
Tube: Piccadilly Circus
In a side street away from the bustle of
Regent Street, this bright café, with polite
French staff, offers 'Les Snacks', including
croque monsieur and a tempting range of
patisserie.

Mon Plaisir *£££*
21 Monmouth Street, WC2
(020-7-836 7243)
Tube: Covent Garden or Leicester Square
A long-established Theatreland restaurant
with the emphasis on traditional bistro
cooking, and a lively, convivial atmosphere.

NORTH

Le Creperie de Hampstead *£*
Corner of Hampstead High Street
and Perrins Lane, NW3
Tube: Hampstead
A Hampstead institution, serving excellent
take-away sweet and savoury crepes, such as
classic Crepe Suzette. Customers stand
mesmerised watching pats of butter sizzle
and melt on the griddles, then a thin pool of
batter spread and metamorphise into a
crepe. Often attracts a queue, particularly
when the pubs close.

Paris-London Café *££*
5 Junction Road, N19
(020-7-561 0330)
Tube: Archway
Tucked away in an unlikely spot just near
Archway Road's busy junction, this small
friendly café attracts a steady stream of
regulars by offering decent bistro dishes –
from Lapin à la Bourguignonne to sautéed
celeriac – at bargain prices.

SOUTH-WEST

Monsieur Max *£££*
133 High Street
Hampton Hill, Surrey
(020-8-979 5546)
Tube: Kew Gardens, then the 68 bus
Run with zest by Max Renzland, this
restaurant offers the chance to try rich,
delicious French food.

COOKBOOKS

Bistro Cooking
Patricia Wells
A wonderfully appetising book of bistro
cooking

Charcuterie and French Pork Cooking
Jane Grigson
A mixture of scholarly knowledge and
practical food writing.

Cooking For Friends
Raymond Blanc
An illustrated cookbook containing recipes
from the chef of Manoir aux Quat' Saisons.

Cuisine Courante
Bruno Loubet
An accessible chef's cookbook.

French Country Cookery
Elizabeth David
Traditional French cooking.

French Provincial Cookery
Elizabeth David
A classic cookbook.

Larousse Gastronomique
A fascinating gastronomic encyclopedia.

**Mastering the Art of French Cookery
(Vols 1 & 2)**,
Simone Beck, Louisette Bertholle & Julia Child
A well-respected, practical textbook.

GREEK LONDON

Continental Stores

The Greek community in London today is about 160,000 strong and largely made up of Greek Cypriots; its growth has been a purely twentieth-century phenomenon. Historically, however, there was a small mainland Greek presence in London which dated back to the eighteenth century. Bishop Timotheus Catsiyannis, of the Cathedral of Aghia Sophia on Moscow Road, has traced back the histories of such prominent Greek families as the Rallis. Pandias Ralli (1793-1865), a prosperous merchant from Chios, came to Britain to expand the family business. He was a leading figure in the early Greek community in Britain, becoming Consul of Greece in 1835.

The Greek community used the Russian Chapel for their religious services and ceremonies until 1837 when a Greek Chapel of Our Saviour was established at 9 Finsbury Circus, where the Ralli brothers had their business. As London's Greek community grew, Pandias felt this chapel to be inadequate and in 1843, proposed building a new church. Seven years later the Greek Church of Our Saviour was opened at London Wall – an historic moment for London's Greek community. This was followed, in 1878, by the completion of the imposing Cathedral of Aghia Sophia in Moscow Road.

The real growth in London's Greek community came much later, as a result of Britain's relations with Cyprus. This strategically important Mediterranean island was leased to the British government in 1878 by the Ottomans, and annexed as a colony by Britain in 1914. During the period of British rule, the lack of opportunities in Cyprus drove many Cypriots to Britain. In the 1930s, the Christian Cypriot Brotherhood was founded in London to offer support to this expat community. The number of Cypriots coming to Britain increased notably after the Second World World and during the 1950s. Many found work as kitchen hands and waiters, and in the garment industry. Soho, with its restaurants and cheap accommodation, was an early focal point. During the late 1940s, however, there was a shift to Camden Town and in 1948 the Greek Cypriots took over the Church of All Saints on Pratt Street. In 1960, Britain withdrew from Cyprus and many of the jobs linked to the naval and military bases disappeared. The economic pull to Britain hit a high point during 1961, when 25,000 Cypriots came to this country. The Turkish invasion of Cyprus in 1974 caused the next major influx, with hundreds of dispossessed refugees fleeing to Britain to seek refuge with family and friends.

During the 1960s the Greek community moved out from Camden, many of them heading north to Turnpike Lane, Wood Green and Palmers Green. Green Lanes, a long road in Haringey, is now a focal point for Greeks, and is lined with greengrocer's shops, kebab houses, bakeries and cafés. Traditionally these cafés were an important contact point for newcomers from Cyprus and continue to act as social centres. Walking down Green Lanes, you pass half-open doors and can glimpse old men sitting around tables, playing cards, reading Greek weeklies or simply watching the world go by.

GREEK CUISINE

The cuisine of ancient Greece, chronicled by the second-century writer Athenaeus, has now been overlayed by other influences. A history of occupation by the Romans, Venetians and Turks has left distinct traces: pasta dishes, kebabs, coffee and honey pastries. There is a clear overlap between Greek and Turkish cooking, especially apparent in Cypriot cooking, and the debate over who originated which dish still continues today. There are also differences: alcohol and pork, prohibited to the Turks under Islam, are used in Greek cooking in dishes like stifatho and afelia. Easter, the most important religious festival in the Greek calendar, is marked by a host of traditional Greek dishes such as mayeritsa: a soup made from lamb head, heart, liver, lungs and intestines; and tsourekia: a braided loaf decorated with a red-dyed, hard-boiled egg, evoking the colour of Christ's blood.

The physical geography of Greece has influenced its cuisine. The long coastline of the mainland and the islands, shared between three seas, means an abundance of fish and seafood dishes. Mediterranean fish soups, such as bouillabaisse, may be Greek in origin. The lack of grazing ground meant that traditionally, meat was scarce and had to be ingeniously spun out: minced and layered with aubergine in moussaka or with macaroni in pastitio, or cubed and skewered in kebabs. Goats and sheep, able to thrive on the rocky hills, were more popular than cattle, with their need for pasture.

From Arcadia onwards this pastoral tradition has continued, and dairy products such as yogurt and cheese still play an important, nutritious part in Greek cookery. The pungent flavour of sheep's, and goat's, milk provides a characteristic sharp note. In agriculture the olive and vine, able to flourish on the rocky hill tops, continue to dominate as they have done for centuries. Their products are essential to Greek cooking: olives on the table, mellow-flavoured olive oil, wine for drinking and cooking and vine leaves for dolmathes. The host of nut trees that thrive in Greece, such as almond, pistachio, walnut and stone pine, play their part, adding flavour and texture to both sweet and savoury dishes.

The lemon, also grown plentifully, sounds one of the keynotes of Greek cooking. Its fresh, sharp flavour characterises dishes such as avgolemono sauce and soup. The fragrant herbs that grow wild on the hill tops are another source of flavour. Athenaeus wrote of herbs being scattered on fish and grilled meat; rigani, or oregano, 'joy of the mountain' is especially popular. The hills are also the source of horta: wild green leaves such as dandelion, wild mustard and chicory, popularly eaten boiled with a dressing.

One Greek influence that has been embraced in kitchens all over the West stems from the Middle Ages. Cooks who entered the monasteries but continued their culinary vocation adopted tall white hats to distinguish themselves from the black-robed and hatted monks – hence the origin of the chef's white hat. The lavish feasts described by Athenaeus or Hesiod the Epicurean in one of the world's first cookbooks are no longer perceived as characteristic Greek cooking. Instead, Greek food is valued for its flavourful simplicity.

GLOSSARY

Bulgar (pourgori): parboiled, cracked wheat grains, available either coarse or finely ground.

Cheeses: anari: a soft cheese, similar to Italian ricotta; feta: a salty, crumbly white cheese made from cow's, sheep's or goat's milk, often stored in brine to retain its freshness; Halloumi: a firm white cheese with a rubbery texture, often flavoured with mint.

Colocassi: a large, brown, fibrous tuber with a distinctive white stump, which is a staple of Cypriot cookery.

Filo: paper-thin pastry, sometimes spelled 'phyllo', used in both sweet and savoury dishes. It's usually available frozen, but occasionally fresh filo can be found. When using filo, be careful not to let it dry out and become brittle.

Glyko: preserved fresh fruit, such as quinces and cherries, in a sweet syrup. Traditionally offered to guests with coffee.

Kataifi: a vermicelli-like pastry, formed by pouring batter through a fine sieve onto a hot surface; usually found frozen.

Loundza: smoked pork loin, a traditional Cypriot Christmas food.

Louvana: a type of vetch, recognisable by its curly tendrils, eaten as a salad leaf.

Mahlepi: the fragrant kernel of the blackcherry stone, sold in husked form and added to sweet yeast breads.

Mastic: the fragrant resin of an evergreen tree, sold in powdered form for use in sweet yeast breads.

Olive oil: in Greek mythology the olive tree was a gift from Athena (the Goddess of Wisdom and Warfare). The rich, fruity oil adds a distinctive flavour to Greek cookery.

Olives: Kalamata, named after the city, are the famous, large, purple-black olives. Tiasis, or cracked olives, are partially-crushed olives which have been marinated, often with olive oil, lemon slices, garlic and cumin seeds.

Ouzo: clear, anise-flavoured liquor, distilled from grapes. When diluted, this potent aperitif becomes white and cloudy and is nicknamed 'lion's milk'.

Parsley: the flat-leafed, flavourful variety known as 'continental parsley' is a basic herb in Greek cookery.

Pasta: dried pasta is a legacy of the Italian influence on Greek cookery. Shapes include macarona, long thick tubes of pasta and manestra, pasta kernels and vermicelli, often cooked with bulgar.

GREEK LONDON

69

Purslane (glysterida): a green salad vegetable with rounded clover-shaped leaves, sometimes called 'Cypriot watercress'.

Retsina: wine with a distinctive resin flavour, traced back to the days when wine was kept in goat skins sealed with pitch.

Rocket (rocca): a green salad leaf with a distinctive peppery flavour, which is now very fashionable.

Sausages: bastourma: dark, short, spiced sausages; loukanika: thin sausages popularly flavoured with allspice, savory and orange peel or coriander seeds.

Savory: a peppery-flavoured herb, which looks similar to thyme.

Tahini: a smooth paste made from pounded sesame seeds.

Tarama: smoked grey mullet roe or, more commonly, cod roe, used to make taramasalata.

Trahani: brown, stubby, crumbly tubes made from fermented cracked wheat and yogurt. They have a tangy flavour and should be soaked before using.

Vine leaves: large, distinctively-shaped leaves, used principally to make dolmathes. Occasionally found fresh but usually preserved in brine, when they need soaking to rinse off excess salt.

Yogurt: thick, creamy Greek yogurt, made from either sheep's or cow's milk.

FOODSHOPS

Greengrocers, filled with fresh salad vegetables, fruit and bunches of herbs (such as mint, continental parsley and dill) and bakers are key shops in the Greek community. At Easter, a hugely important festival, the bakers are filled with traditional specialities such as Lambropsomo, a sweet bread decorated with red-dyed, hard-boiled eggs symbolising Christ. In London the Greek Cypriot community live amicably side by side with the Turkish Cypriot community, with, roughly speaking, the Turnpike Lane end of Green Lanes being Greek and the Stoke Newington end, Turkish.

NORTH

Clocktower Store
52 The Broadway, N8
(020-8-348 7845)
Tube: Finsbury Park, then the W7 bus
Open: Mon-Fri 8.30am-7pm;
Sat 8.30am-6pm; Sun 10am-5pm
This friendly, bustling greengrocer's, just by Crouch End's Clock Tower, offers an excellent range of fruit and veg, from bunches of fresh herbs to huge watermelons.

Andreas Michli & Sons
405-411 St Ann's Road, N15
(020-8-802 0188)
BR: Harringay Green Lanes
Open: Mon-Thur 9.30am-7.30pm;
Fri 9.30am-8.30pm; Sat 9.30am-7.30pm;
Sun 11am-3.30pm
Tucked away just off Green Lanes, this small, characterful parade of shops offer everything from foodstuffs to barbecue equipment and Greek statuary. Andreas takes particular pride in the fresh produce, which includes delights such as bergamot lemons, sweet, juicy unwaxed oranges and the bunches of the fresh herbs essential to Greek cooking.

Halepi
24 Grand Parade
Green Lanes, N4
Tube: Manor House
Open: Mon-Sun 9.30am-8pm
This Greek bakery, which is around 25 years old, is something of an institution, and especially famous among the Greek community for its monumental, multi-tiered, lavishly-iced wedding cakes, a display of which is kept upstairs.

Milia Wholesale Co Ltd
200-202 St Anns Road, N15
(020-8-802 7654)
Tube: Seven Sisters
Open: Mon-Sat 9am-8pm
The bright blue walls signal a Greek presence here on this long main road. Milia specialises in everything for Greek barbecues – from sacks of charcoal by the door to savoury bastourma and louganika sausages and halloumi cheese, plus stacks of Greek and Cypriot beers.

Tony's Continental Stores
140 High Road, N2
(020-8-444 5545)
Tube: East Finchley
Open: Mon-Fri 8am-7pm; Sat 8am-6.30pm;
Sun 10am-1pm
From watermelons and figs in the summer to quinces and huge field mushrooms in the autumn, there is always a good range of produce at this self-service greengrocer's, run with friendly courtesy by the Athanasiou family.

GREEK LONDON

71

GREEK LONDON

WEST

Adamou
126 Chiswick High Road, W4
(020-8-994 0752)
Tube: Turnham Green
Open: Mon-Sun 8.30am-6.45pm
This Chiswick institution has an attractive array of produce outside: from rocket and avocados to bunches of flowers. Inside, there is a good range of general groceries: olives, pasta, cheeses and cured meats.

Athenian Grocery
16a Moscow Road, W2
(020-7-229 6280)
Tube: Bayswater
Open: Mon-Sat 8.30am-7pm;
Sun 9.30am-1pm
Down the road from St Sophia is this charming corner shop, its blue-painted exterior and boxes of vegetables striking an attractive Mediterranean note. Established

for around 40 years, its stock includes seasonal items such as green almonds and fresh vine leaves, as well as basic staples. Banter is the name of the game and insults are genially exchanged with regular customers, but service is friendly and heavy bags are carried out to waiting cars.

SOUTH-EAST

Andreas
18 Lordship Lane, SE22
(020-8-299 2214)
BR: East Dulwich,
then the 40, 176, 185, or 484 bus
Open: Mon-Sat 9am-9pm; Sun 10am-8pm
Crates of fresh fruit and vegetables such as colocassi and aubergines mark the presence of this roomy Cypriot grocers. The deli-counter is crammed with Greek cakes, cheese and cured meats and there is a good range of basic stock.

EATING PLACES

NORTH LONDON

Daphne £££
83 Bayham Street, NW1
(020-7-267 7322)
Tube: Camden Town
A pleasant and convivial restaurant offering decent Greek food, popular for both romantic tête-à-têtes and parties of friends.

Lemonia £££
89 Regent's Park Road, NW1
(020-7-586 7454)
Tube: Chalk Farm
With its lively atmosphere, friendly staff and fresh-tasting food this is everyone's idea of what a Greek restaurant should be and accordingly, pulls in the revellers.

Nontas £££
16 Camden High Street, NW1
(020-7-387 4579)
Tube: Camden Town
Rustically decorated with dark wood and old family photographs, Nontas combines an Ouzerie area, in which to drink and snack, with a restaurant offering good simple, Cyriot food at reasonable prices. There is also a pretty little courtyard which is a popular dining area during fine weather. Helpful relaxed staff, plus two friendly cats, make it a pleasant place in which to while away an evening.

Vrisiaki £££
73 Myddleton Road, N22
(020-8-889 8760)
Tube: Bounds Green
Warmly recommended by Cypriot friends, at first sight this looks solely like a take-away kebab house. Venture in, however, past the busy charcoal grills and it opens into a large, busy restaurant. Those with gargantuan appetites should opt for mezedes, a seemingly never-ending array of dishes, starting with nibbles such as tahini and cracked olives and working up via seafood to a platter of grilled meats.

WEST

Kalamares Mega £££
76-78 Inverness Mews, W2
(020-7-727 9122)
Tube: Bayswater or Queensway

Kalamares Micro £££
66 Inverness Mews, W2
(020-7-727 5082)
Tube: Bayswater or Queensway
These two popular restaurants offer the chance to sample Greek food, as opposed to more widely available Greek Cypriot food, and have a specials list. Mega is the more expensive of the two, while Micro is unlicensed so that diners can bring their own wine.

COOKBOOKS

A Book of Mediterranean Food
Elizabeth David
A knowledgeable and evocative book which, although not solely about Greek cookery, captures the flavours of the Mediterranean.

The Cooking of Greece and Turkey
Rena Salaman
A straightforward, illustrated cookbook from Sainsbury's, full of tasty recipes.

Mediterranean Cookery
Claudia Roden
A well-written and attractive book, dealing with the Mediterranean as a whole.

The Taste of Cyprus
Gilli Davies
A charmingly-written cookbook, combining evocative personal memories with straightforward recipes.

ITALIAN LONDON

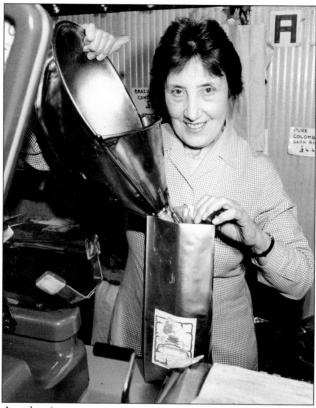

Angelucci

Italian links with London date back to the Roman invasion in AD 43 and the creation of a settlement called 'Londinium'. Over subsequent centuries Italians came to live in London, but particularly so in the first half of the nineteenth century when waves of political refugees arrived in the capital. The community continued to grow through the turbulent times of Italian unification and war with Austria – by 1900 there were around 10,000 Italians in London.

The historical Italian quarter, founded in the mid-nineteenth century, was in Clerkenwell and Holborn, known to outsiders as 'Little Italy' and to its residents as 'The Hill'. The nickname The Hill came from two important streets in the community: Back Hill and Eyre Street Hill. St Peter's Church was the community's focal point, erected in 1864 with money donated by Italian immigrants; its importance in celebrating and commemorating the births, lives and deaths of the Italian community continues to this day. Although the Italian population has now dispersed from Clerkenwell, the legacy of this period is still visible in the area around King's Cross and Holborn where red, white and green signs over barber's, cafés and shops patriotically signal Italy.

red, white and green signs over barber's, cafés and shops patriotically signal Italy. Every year on the first Sunday after July 16th, the Feast Day of Our Lady of Mount Carmel, a religious procession in her honour takes place through Clerkenwell from St Peter's, followed by a 'sagra' or fete. One of the few religious processions to take place in London, it has been enacted since the 1880s and older Italians have fond memories of attending it as children. Even today, the procession draws Italians back to Clerkenwell from all over Britain. There is a great sense of community, with the different generations all present and participating. Stalls are set up on the streets selling delicious Italian snacks such as polenta e salsiccie (cornmeal and sausages), freshly-roasted porchetta (pork) and slices of savoury tarts, with glasses of wine adding to the celebratory atmosphere.

The other traditional Italian area in London was Soho, which also saw an influx of Italians in the 1860s. Despite the internment of Italian residents as 'enemy aliens' during the Second World War and the tragic death in 1940 of 470 Italian internees being deported to Canada when the Arandora Star was sunk by the Germans, the Italian community continued to maintain its links with Britain. In the 1950s and 1960s, during the espresso bar boom, a wave of immigrants, mostly from the south of Italy, came to London seeking work and settled in Soho as waiters and restauranteurs.

ITALIAN CUISINE

Italian cuisine is very much a regional cuisine; the different parts of Italy, united only in the last century, have their own dishes and even their own ingredients. The historical divide between the prosperous, industrial north and the poor, rural south also extended to foodstuffs. Rice, polenta made with cornmeal, and fresh egg pasta were the staples of the north while in the south factory-made, dried durum wheat pasta was eaten. Cooking fats varied: the north used butter, middle-Italy pig fat, and the south, olive oil. With the post-war migration of labour from south to north and the growth of mass-production, regional eating patterns became less rigid. Today the Mediterranean diet, stemming from the south, is valued for its health-giving qualities. Dried pasta and olive oil, low in saturated fats, are now eaten throughout Italy.

Despite this blurring of the north-south divide, regional characteristics are still apparent. Tuscan cuisine comprises of rustic, peasant food such as bean soup (the Tuscans are nick-named 'mangiafagioli', bean-eaters), bruschetta and charcoal-grilled meat such as bistecca fiorentina, a T-bone steak traditionally from the Val di Chiana. Rice dishes are still popular in the north, where rice was traditionally grown, and in Lombardy you find risotto alla Milanese, flavoured with saffron, wine and stock. Roman cuisine is that of the 'quinto quarto', the fifth quarter, with the poor eating what was left after the rich had eaten, hence strongly-flavoured offal dishes. Sicily has a rich, varied culinary inheritance due to a history of invasions by the Greeks, Romans, Arabs and Normans. The Arab legacy is particularly noticeable, with sultanas, aubergines, pistachio nuts and spices being popular ingredients in Sicily.

Italian cooking is noted for its emphasis on clear, simple flavours. Good ingredients are the key to Italian cooking and seasonality is valued. Foods continue to be associated with the regions, towns or villages that have traditionally produced that ingredient: the best radicchio from Treviso, with its annual radicchio festival; balsamic vinegar from Modena; prosciutto from Parma or San Daniele; fontina cheese from Val d'Aosta; and costly white truffles from Alba.

ITALIAN LONDON

75

GLOSSARY

Baccala: pungent salted, dried cod which needs soaking before cooking.

Balsamic vinegar: an aromatic brown vinegar made from wine must and historically from Modena. Traditionally-matured balsamic vinegar is very expensive while cheaper, commercially produced balsamic vinegar compresses the maturing process into a few years.

Ciabatta: a flavourful, distinctively-textured bread, named after a houseshoe because of its flattened, oval shape.

Colomba: a dove-shaped cake similar to panettone, but traditionally eaten at Easter.

Foccacia: a flat, salty bread flavoured with olive oil and sometimes additionally with rosemary, onions or sage; known as schiacciata in Tuscany.

Fontina: a semi-soft cow's milk cheese, traditionally from Val d'Aosta, and famously used to make fonduta, a fondue flavoured with white truffles.

Marscapone: an extremely rich cream cheese, an essential ingredient for the popular dessert tiramisu.

Mortadella: a large pink sausage, traditionally from Bologna, flavoured with peppercorns, garlic and pistachios. It can be eaten like a salami or used in cooking.

Mozzarella: a bland white cheese with a rubbery texture that is famously used on pizzas. Buffalo's milk mozzarella is more expensive than the more easily found cow's milk version. Baby mozzarellas are called 'bocconcini'.

Olive oil: a key ingredient in Italian cooking, olive oil is labelled according to its acidity levels. Extra Virgin must have no more than 1% acidity. As with wine, different regions produce different-flavoured olive oils, with Tuscan olive oil being famously piquant.

Pancetta: the Italian equivalent of bacon, this is made from the same cut of meat – pig belly.

Panettone: a light, brioche-style cake, containing sultanas, traditionally given at Christmas time, which is when the Italian delis stock several varieties.

Parmesan: the best-known Italian cheese and also the largest and longest-matured cheese produced in Italy, this hard-grating cheese comes traditionally from around Parma. Grana padano is a similar cheese produced in Lombardy. Buy chunks of Parmesan and keep them refrigerated, wrapped in foil, to be used as required.

Pasta: this famous Italian staple comes both fresh and dried and in a multiplicity of forms. Fresh pasta, made with eggs, can be bought ready-made from delicatessens. Dried pasta should be made from durum wheat and popular Italian brands include Barilla and Da Cecco.

Pecorino: a hard sheep's milk cheese. Pecorino Romano is most commonly found but there is also Pecorino Sardo, from Sardinia, and Toscana, from Tuscany.

Pine nuts: small ivory-coloured kernels from the stone pine tree, with a distinctive flavour.

Polenta: a Northern Italian staple made from maize, polenta flour is available in fine or coarse versions. Pre-cooked polenta flour, scorned by purists, is also available.

Porcini: wild Boletus mushrooms, prized for their flavour and priced accordingly. Dried porcini mushrooms, often in pieces, are easily found, while fresh porcini are much rarer.

Prosciutto Crudo: the most famous of these salt-cured hams is Parma ham, cured for 14 months. San Daniele, cured for 12 months, is considered another fine prosciutto.

Ricotta: a light, bland sheep's whey cheese, drained in baskets which give it its distinctive woven markings. It is used in both sweet and savoury dishes.

Rocket: known as 'rucola', this peppery, jagged leaf is increasingly available as a chic salad leaf. Italians are fond of pointing out that in Italy it grows wild as a weed.

Salami: ready-to-eat, salt-cured sausages, available in a range of sizes and flavours, such as fine-textured Milano or finocchiona, flavoured with fennel.

Salsiccie: Italian sausages, usually made from pork. Luganega is a mild sausage from Lombardy, sold in long narrow coils, while in the South chilli is often added as a flavouring.

Sun-dried tomatoes: as their name suggests, these are dried tomatoes, available either in their dry state or preserved in olive oil.

Truffles: these rare tubers with their overwhelming and distinctive flavour are astronomically expensive, especially when sold fresh. White truffles from Alba are particularly prized. Tinned and bottled truffles are available as is truffle-flavoured olive oil.

ITALIAN LONDON

Ciabatta

FOODSHOPS

T he older Italian delicatessens in London grew out of the community's needs, starting as everyday cornershops supplying foods that had to be specially imported. In some cases the shop acted as an informal community centre, lending money, explaining English laws and providing advice. As the Italian community have become assimilated into British life this role has disappeared. With Italian food now enjoying a huge wave of fashionable popularity, newer, more upmarket delicatessens are entering the market and are aimed as much at the English as the Italians.

CENTRAL

Angelucci
23b Frith Street, W1
(020-7-437 5889)
Tube: Leicester Square or
Tottenham Court Road
Open: Mon-Wed 9am-5pm;
Thur 9am-1pm; Fri-Sat 9am-5pm
Founded in 1929 by Signore Angelucci and still run by the family, this tiny shop smells enticingly of roasted coffee – it sells 36 varieties. The most popular is Mokital, for cappuccinos and espressos, which is freshly ground as required in one of their huge old coffee-grinding machines. If you want to sample Mokital, drop into Bar Italia next door and have one of their much-famed espressos or cappuccinos. Over the decades, customers have included General du Gaulle and numerous Dire Straits fans, drawn by the reference to Angelucci's in the song *The Wild West End.*

I Camisa & Son
61 Old Compton Street, W1
(020-7-437 7610/4686)
Tube: Leicester Square or
Tottenham Court Road
Open: Mon-Sat 9am-6pm
On this bustling Soho thoroughfare, Gaby presides genially over this classic Italian deli. Established around thirty years ago, this small shop has a seemingly perpetual queue of loyal regulars, attracted by the quality of the cheeses (including excellent Parmesan),

meats and delicious home-marinated olives. Fresh pasta includes pappardelle and there are homemade sauces such as pesto, lepre (hare) and porcini.

Carluccio's
28a Neal Street, WC2
(020-7-240 1487)
Tube: Covent Garden
Open: Mon-Thur 11am-7pm;
Fri 10am-7pm; Sat 10am-6pm
Set up by restauranteur and funghiphile Antonio Carluccio (also of the neighbouring Neal Street Restaurant) and his wife Priscilla, this sleek shop offers an appetising selection of regional Italian foods, including a counter of ready-made dishes and fresh pasta. Everything, from the Calabrian stuffed figs to the rustic loaves of bread, is beautifully packaged and presented. Naturally, there is also a fine seasonal range of fresh wild mushrooms and truffles.

Fratelli Camisa
53 Charlotte Street, W1
(020-7-255 1240)
Tube: Goodge Street
Open: Mon-Sat 9am-6pm
This large, well-established shop stocks fresh pasta and several cheeses and keeps a fine variety of olive oils, from the everyday to the exclusive.

I Camisa

Gastronomeria Italia

8 Upper Tachbrook Street, SW1
(020-7-834 2767)
Tube: Pimlico or Victoria
Open: Mon-Fri 9am-6pm; Sat 9am-5pm
This homely delicatessen is well patronised
by Italians and Spaniards from the local
community. As well as a good basic stock of
Italian ingredients, they sell tasty Italian
snacks to cater to the lunchtime market.

Gazzano G. & Son

169 Farringdon Road, EC1
(020-7-837 1586)
Tube: Farringdon
Open: Mon & Sat 8am-5pm;
Tue-Fri 8am-6pm; Sun 10.30am-2pm
This venerable shop was set up in 1901 in
the heart of the Clerkenwell Italian
community, and even today you are likely
to hear Signore Gazzano bellowing in
Italian across the street to a passing friend.
The shop retains its down-to-earth roots
with clearly-arranged stock: salamis and
sausages in one counter, cheeses in another,
and dried pasta along the wall.

Lina Stores

18 Brewer Street, W1
(020-7-437 6482)
Tube: Leicester Square, Oxford Circus or
Piccadilly Circus
Open: Mon-Fri 7am-5.45pm; Sat 7am-5pm
The pistachio-coloured facade and the
1930s lettering tell you this is a well
established shop. Customers return as much
for the friendly, leisurely atmosphere as for
the delicious food. It is famous for its
excellent fresh pasta, made on the premises
every morning. The speciality is pumpkin
tortelloni, a dish from Piacanza where the
Filippi family come from. Recent additions
to the pasta range include four cheese
tortelloni and squid's ink tagliatelle.
Groceries are wide-ranging – you feel you
could ask for any Italian ingredient and it
would be conjured up.

La Picena

5 Walton Street, SW3
(020-7-584 6573)
Tube: Knightsbridge
Open: Mon-Fri 9am-7.30pm; Sat 9am-5.30pm
Tucked away behind Harrods is this
refreshingly down-to-earth 18 year-old
delicatessen. It is crammed full of good-
quality Italian provisions including fresh
pasta and excellent homemade pasta sauces.

L. Terroni & Sons

138-40 Clerkenwell Road, EC1
(020-7-837 1712)
Tube: Chancery Lane or Farringdon
Open: Mon-Wed & Fri 9am-5.45pm;
Thur 9am-2pm; Sat 9am-3pm;
Sun 10.30am-2pm
Next to St Peter's Church – a focal point
for London's Italian community – Terroni's
was established in 1890 in the heart of Little
Italy. The large shop retains its grocery store
roots, offering a good selection of Italian
foodstuffs, and is a popular stopping-off
point after the church's Sunday service.

NORTH

Amici Delicatessen

78 High Road, N2
(020-8-444 2932)
Tube: East Finchley
Open: Mon-Sat 8am-7pm; Sun 10am-1pm
A friendly, basic Italian deli, which draws in
a lunchtime crowd for its paninis and
freshly-made espressos.

Il Boungustaio

90 Stroud Green Road, N4
(020-7-263 5705)
Tube: Finsbury Park
Open: Mon-Sat 8am-8pm, Sun 8am-5pm
A small, friendly, down-to-earth shop,
combining a sandwich bar, deli section and
newsagents. Customers return for the
generously filled panini – such as pesto and
parma ham in ciabatta and the Italian gelati.

A. Ferrari

48 Cross Street, N1
(020-7-226 1951)
Tube: Angel or Highbury & Islington
Open: Mon-Fri 8am-6pm; Sat 8am-6pm;
Sun 9.30am-1.30pm
Tucked away in an Islington side-street, this small family-run deli is now in its 30th year. The stock is basic and unpretentious, with a good range of salamis, De Cecco and Barilla dried pasta and traditional cakes such as panettone at Christmas.

Giacobazzi's Delicatessen

150 Fleet Road, NW3
(020-7-267 7222)
BR: Hampstead Heath
Open: Mon-Fri 9.30am-7pm; Sat 9am-6pm
The speciality here is ready-made fresh foods, of which there is an appetising display. The dishes are made on the premises by Raffaele Giacobazzi, who, acccording to his wife Renata, has a particular penchant for chargrilled vegetables ranging from radicchio to onions in balsamic vinegar. Homemade pasta, freshly made every day, includes upmarket treats such as gorgonzola and walnut and porcini, and white truffle tortellini.

Limoncello

402 St John Street, EC1
(020-7-713 1678)
Tube: Angel
Open: Mon-Fri 8.30am-7pm;
Sat 9.30am-2.30pm
This new-wave traiteur-cum-deli, snazzily decorated in lemon yellow and dark blue, offers freshly-cooked Mediterranean dishes to take away, ranging from Italian sausage sandwiches to stuffed swordfish. There is a small stock of foodstuffs, such as excellent breads, jams, pulses, wines and spirits.

Monte's

23 Canonbury Lane, N1
(020-7-354 4335)
Tube: Highbury & Islington
Open: Mon-Fri 10am-7pm; Sat 9.30am-6pm
This is a New Wave Italian deli, with mauve walls, black glossy floor tiles, gleaming metal shelving and jazz playing in the background. Stock is distinctly upmarket, from large bowlfuls of marinated olives and insalata di mare to fresh funghi ravioli. Groceries include several olive oils, balsamic vinegars and polentas.

Mauro's Deli

229 Muswell Hill Broadway, N10
(020-8-883 2848)
Bus: 134 or W7
Open: Tue-Sat 10am-7pm; Sun 11am-4pm
An eye-catching window display of colourful homemade pasta demonstrates the shop's speciality. In addition to the large pasta range there are homemade sauces and a selection of basic foodstuffs.

Olga Stores

30 Penton Street, N1
(020-7-837 5467)
Tube: Angel
Open: Mon-Fri 9am-8pm; Sat 9am-7pm;
Sun 10am-2pm
Run by the charming and knowledgeable Aida, this upmarket deli (now in its tenth year) caters to its Islington clientele with a wide selection of foodstuffs, from marinated olives to breads. Bestselling items include Aida's homemade lasagne and her huge range of sauces, from tomato-based arrabiata and vongole to pesto.

Saponara

23 Prebend Street, N1
(020-7-226 2771)
Tube: Angel
Open: Mon-Fri 8am-7.30pm; Sat 9am-7pm
Run with friendly courtesy by brothers Marco and Vincenzo Saponara, this roomy

ITALIAN LONDON

81

deli-cum-bar offers a classic Italian mixture of excellent foodstuffs, from huge bunches of truly fresh basil, rosemary and flat-leaf parsley to their home-marinated olives 'arrabiata'. Specialities include homemade pesto ("made the traditional way with pine nuts, not other nuts"), pecorino with truffles, fine Italian wines and superior fresh pasta from Italy – including gnocchi with porcini and artichoke tortellini. There are even a couple of tables at which to enjoy a cappuccino and panino, al' Italiano.

Salvino Ltd
47 Brecknock Road, N7
(020-7-267 5305)
Bus: 29, 253 or 10
Open: Mon-Sat 9am-6.30pm
A pleasant shop run by the Salvino brothers. As they import Italian food their stock is above average, with a good selection of meat, wines and aperitivos.

SOUTH-EAST

Delicatessen Piacenza
2 Brixton Road, SW9
(020-7-735 2121)
Tube: Oval
Open: Mon-Fri 9am-6.30pm; Sat 9am-6pm; Sun 10am-1.30pm

There has been an Italian deli on the site for around 20 years. This small shop stocks a good range of basics plus some fancy fresh pastas.

La Gastronomeria
135 Half Moon Lane, SE24
(020-7-274 1034)
BR: Herne Hill or North Dulwich
Open: Mon-Sat 9am-6pm
This friendly well-stocked Italian deli offers customers a good range of basic groceries, from Italian dried pastas to packets of biscotti. Popular items on the deli counter include the homemade pastas and antipasti, made by their sister shop in West Dulwich.
Also at: *86 Park Hall Road, SE21*
(020 87660494)

SOUTH-WEST LONDON

Luigi's Delicatessen
349 Fulham Road, SW10
(020-7-352 7739)
Tube: Fulham Broadway
Open: Mon-Fri 9am-9.30pm; Sat 9am-7pm
This roomy, cheerful delicatessen attracts a steady stream of loyal customers. The stock is extensive and high-quality: 40 olive oils and over 300 Italian wines, spirits and aperitivos. There is an appetising display of homemade sauces and dishes.

Rosticceria Roma
152 Streatham Hill, SW2
(020-8-674 1901)
BR: Streatham Hill
Bus: 60, 115, 118, 133, 137, 159
Open: Mon–Sat 10am-7pm
An appetising selection of homemade dishes such as arancine (rice balls with mozzarella) fill the windows of this friendly delicatessen. There is an excellent range of stock including breads, cheeses, wines and dried pasta.

Salumeria Estense

837 Fulham Road, SW6
(020-7-731 7643)
Tube: Parsons Green
Open: Mon-Fri 10am-7.30pm;
Sat 10am-5.30pm
Warmly recommended by Italian food
historian Anna del Conte, this pretty,
friendly delicatessen run by Mr and Mrs
Gorini has stylish stock including upmarket
olive oils, vinegars and wines. Pasta is
freshly made on the premises, including
paglia e fieno, and there is a range of chargrilled vegetables and excellent homemade
sauces such as rocket pesto "made only in
the summer when it has flavour".

Salumeria Napoli

69 Northcote Road, SW11
(020-7-228 2445)
BR: Clapham Junction
Open: Mon-Sat 9am-6pm
A friendly corner shop with an appetising
deli-counter containing olives, homemade
red and green pesto sauces and a good
selection of salamis and cured meats.

Tony's Continental Delicatessen

South Lambeth Road, SW8
(020-7-582 0766)
Tube: Vauxhall
Open: Mon-Fri 7am-6.30pm;
Sat 7am-5.30pm
This down-to-earth corner deli has been
serving the people of Vauxhall for around 10
years now. On offer are deli basics, from
dried pasta to chunks of Parmesan. There is
fresh Italian bread and also panini, made up
with salami and cheese from the deli counter.

Valentina

210 Upper Richmond Road West, SW14
(020-8-392 9127)
BR: Mortlake
Open: Mon-Fri 9am-7pm; Sat 8.30am-6pm;
Sun 9.30am-3pm

The Borfecchia's attractive, friendly
delicatessen has a loyal local following.
Particularly popular are the home-prepared
dishes, from grilled vegetables to lasagne and
parmigiani. There is a good range of grocery
items including fresh truffles when they are
in season.

WEST LONDON

Speck

2 Holland Park Terrace, W11
(020-7-229 7005)
Tube: Holland Park
Open: Mon-Fri 9am-8.30pm; Sat 8.30am-7pm
This small, sleek shop offers upmarket stock,
from an attractive display of home-made
dishes such as marinated grilled vegetables to
a good assortment of balsamic vinegars and
fine olive oils.

MAIL ORDER

Fratelli Camisa

Unit 3
Lismirrane Industrial Park
Elstree Road,
Elstree
Herts WD6 3EE
(020-8–207 5919)

ITALIAN LONDON

EATING PLACES

L ondon's Italian restaurant scene has recently undergone a transformation. A whole new wave of elegant, smart and expensive restaurants have opened up offering authentic, delicious and regional Italian cooking – rather than the 'Britalian' fare on offer before.

CENTRAL

Bar Italia £
22 Frith Street, W1
(020-7-437 4520)
Tube: Leicester Square or
Tottenham Court Road
Despite its status as a cult place for a late night espresso, Bar Italia remains thankfully down-to-earth, complete with fruit machines, a giant video screen for Italian football and Rocky Marciano glowering down from behind the bar.

Coffee Gallery £
23 Museum Street, WC1
(020-7-436 0455)
Tube: Holborn, Russell Square or
Tottenham Court Road
This charming, colourful café sells delicious freshly-prepared Italian sandwiches, salads and soups using flavourful ingredients such as aubergines, artichokes and rocket.

Costa Coffee Boutiques £
(several branches throughout London)
Set up as outlets to sell roasted coffee, Costa Coffee branches are decked out in gleaming marble and mirrors. The coffee is excellent and can be accompanied by Italian-style panini or cakes.

Kettners *££*
29 Romilly Street, W1
(020-7-437 6437)
Tube: Leicester Square or
Tottenham Court Road
Owned by Pizza Express creator Peter
Boizot, this historic building is now the
grandest pizza restaurant in town.

Pizza Express *££*
29 Wardour Street, W1
(020-7-734 7215)
Tube: Leicester Square or
Tottenham Court Road
Opened in 1965, this was the first restaurant
in Peter Boizot's successful Pizza Express
chain, all of which offer excellent Italian-
style pizza with thin, crispy bases and tasty
toppings. Consult a phone book for your
nearest branch.

Spiga *£££*
84-86 Wardour Street, W1
(020-7-734 3444)
Tube: Tottenham Court Road
A smart, rather hectic restaurant offering the
chance to sample excellent pasta dishes (such
as linguine with crab and chilli) and
authentically thin-crust, wood-fired pizzas
with sophisticated toppings.

La Spighetta *£££*
43 Blandford Street, W1
(020-7-486 7340)
Tube: Baker Street
Linked to La Spiga and Zafferano, this offers
authentically Italian pasta and pizza.

Zafferano *££££*
15 Lowndes Street, SW1
(020-7-235 5800)
Tube: Knightsbridge
Georgio Locatelli's justly-praised restaurant
is an elegant affair, as one would expect
from its Knightsbridge location, offering
very fine Italian food indeed: imaginative
antipasti, superb fresh pasta, excellent meat

and seafood and delectable desserts. The
pleasant, impeccable service matches the
food, making dining here a truly enjoyable
experience.

NORTH

Florians *££*
4 Topsfield Parade
Middle Lane, N8
(020-8-348 8348)
Bus: W7
A pleasant, roomy bar-cum-restaurant
offering regional Italian cooking,
predominantly from the north, such as
Venetian fish pie.

Marine Ices *££*
8 Haverstock Hill, NW3
(020-7-485 3132)
Tube: Chalk Farm
A nautically-named gelateria set up by
Gaetano Mansi in 1930. He had been a
fruiterer and the family myth goes that he
began making water-ices from left over
fruit. The family business prides itself on its
range of flavourful Italian ice creams, using
ingredients such as Van Houten cocoa,
dark-roasted Mocha and fresh mangoes and
oranges. Grander desserts such as tartufo and
cassata Siciliana have traditionally been
brought for many a family occasion by
London's Italian community. There is also a
relaxed family-friendly restaurant area
serving good tasty pizza and pasta, such as
spaghetti alle vongole.

La Porchetta Pizzeria *££*
147 Stroud Green Road, N4
(020-7-281 2892)
Tube: Finsbury Park
The gargantuan, flavoursome and thin-based
pizzas on offer here ensure a busy, bustling
atmosphere.

ITALIAN LONDON

Refreshment House £

Golders Hill Park
North End Road, NW3
Tube: Golders Green
Popular with families with young children
and old age pensioners alike, this large
Italian cafe serves up cappuccini, panini and
a few pasta dishes. The star attraction,
however, is their own gelati – fresh-tasting
ice creams from refreshing melon to sweet,
moreish marron, studded with pieces of
marrons glacés.

SOUTH

La Famiglia ££££

7 Langton Street, SW10
(020-7-351 0761)
Bus: 11, 22 or 31
An elegant but expensive restaurant,
popular with Italians, which offers well-
executed, predominantly Tuscan cooking.

King's Road Café £

Habitat
208 King's Road, SW3
(020-7-351 1211)
Tube: Sloane Square
This bright and airy café, run by the same
people who run Bloomsbury's Coffee
Gallery, offers the same tasty mix of freshly-
made salads, delicious soups and imaginative
sandwiches.

Pizza Metro ££

64 Battersea Park Rise, SW11
(020-7-228 3812)
BR: Clapham Junction
Neapolitan food at its best, from aubergine
parmigiana to mozzarella in carrozza, and
splendid wood oven-baked pizzas.

Pizzeria Castello ££

20 Walworth Road, SE1
(020-7-703 2556)
Tube: Elephant and Castle
An appetising waft of garlic signals this
popular pizzeria. Regulars return for the
excellent crisp pizzas and lively service.

WEST

Assaggi ££££

The Chepstow
39 Chepstow Place, W2
(020-7-792 5501)
Tube: Notting Hill Gate
In an unlikely setting above a pub this small
restaurant is noted for its flavourful,
authentic Italian food.

Riva £££

169 Church Road, SW13
(020-8-748 0434)
BR: Barnes Bridge
A restaurant pioneer of regional Italian
cooking, Riva continues to offer
imaginative and tasty dishes in an elegant
setting, and has a loyal clientele.

The River Cafe £££££

Thames Wharf
Rainville Road, W6
(020-7-381 8824)
Tube: Hammersmith
Cool and stylish, this upmarket and
expensive restaurant originally opened as a
canteen for workers in the Richard Rogers-
designed wharf complex. The ingredients
are Italian, with the emphasis on good
quality, freshly and flavourfully interpreted
by Ruthie Rogers and Rose Gray. Two
bestselling cookbooks and a television series
have ensured that its fame has spread far and
wide.

COOKBOOKS

Eco Brixton Ltd   £
4 Market Row, SW9
(020-7-738 3021)
Tube: Brixton
Tucked away amongst the hustle and bustle
of Brixton Market, this tiny, relaxed pizzeria
offers authentic Italian thin-based pizzas,
generously topped with gourmet treats like
fresh rocket or roasted red peppers. Food is
served until 5pm in the afternoon.
Also at: *Eco, 162 Clapham High Street, SW4*
(020-7-622 6848)

Al Bocconvino   ££
10b Kew Green
Kew Gardens, TW9
(020-8-940 6424)
Tube: Kew Gardens
A classic Italian trattoria (much-loved by
locals), presided over with great charm by its
owner Franco and offering excellent
versions of classics such as melt-in-the-
mouth fegato alla salvia, melanzane
parmigiana, and light and crisp battered
courgettes.

The Classic Food of Northern Italy
Gastronomy of Italy
Secrets of an Italian Kitchen
Anna del Conte
The first book is a lovingly-written look at
the foods of her home region, the second an
authoritative encyclopedia of Italian food
and the third, an imaginative cookbook
arranged by ingredients.

Italian Food
Elizabeth David
Although first published in 1954, her
comments on the essence of Italian cookery
remain perceptive and valid. A classic.

A Table in Tuscany
Leslie Forbes
An attractively-illustrated evocation of
Tuscan cooking.

Italian Regional Cookery
Valentina Harris
A lively and informative recipe book.

The Classic Italian Cookbook
The Second Classic Italian Cookbook
Marcella's Kitchen
Marcella Hazan
Three wonderful cookbooks by a highly
respected author: a great source of
knowledgeable writing about Italian
cookery and delicious recipes. Essential.

The Food of Italy
Claudia Roden
A beautifully-written guide to the regions of
Italy and their cookery; both evocative and
useable.

ITALIAN LONDON

JAPANESE LONDON

T he Japanese presence in London is a comparatively recent phenomenon. Japan's deliberate cultural isolation for hundreds of years was broken down in the seventeenth century by Portuguese traders and missionaries, but contact with the West remained limited. It was during Japan's post-Second World War business boom, as the country restored and developed its economy, that a community developed in London. It is primarily a business community, consisting of families on postings for large companies and banks. The temporary nature of most of these postings has kept the community transitory and relatively rootless. Social life, as in Japan, is conducted largely round the golf course and at business lunches.

It used to be said that the Japanese lived on the Northern Line, which provided access to all their needs, from the City for work to the leafy suburbs of Finchley and Golders Green for housing, with much-valued golf courses nearby. The presence of the Oriental City shopping plaza at Colindale was prompted by the growth of this North London community. The shifting of the Japanese School to Acton, however, has opened up a new area of suburban London for the Japanese community and the Northern Line is no longer the sole axis. The past decade has also seen a growing Japanese presence in the West End, with shops opening to cater for the influx of prosperous Japanese tourists.

JAPANESE CUISINE

T his highly refined cuisine, which developed in isolation for hundreds of years, is both aesthetic and ascetic. In Japan's codified society, a meticulously disciplined approach governs food preparation as well as other aspects of life. Presentation is all-important: small portions of foods are carefully arranged, delighting both the eye and the palate. Nouvelle cuisine borrowed greatly from Japanese culinary aesthetics.

'Kisetsukan' is the Japanese term for a sympathy with nature, important in Japanese culture. Dishes are designed to echo nature, perhaps creating a minature landscape or simply a natural gracefulness. A great value is placed on freshness and seasonality. Fish and vegetables, two key foodstuffs, are at their best fresh. Sashimi, raw fish served with a dipping sauce, epitomises this emphasis. Even though modern preserving techniques have robbed seasonality of its practical imperative, it continues to be valued. There is a whole range of dishes, such as cherry blossom rice or oden, eaten in appropriate months and seasons, with even preserved ingredients such as pickles and miso pastes changing according to the time of year. The flavour of individual ingredients is emphasised in the cooking rather than disguised. Even a Japanese stew retains the separate flavours of ingredients rather than blending them into a whole.

The range of seasonings in Japanese food is limited, falling into three broad categories: salty (provided by shoyu and dashi), sweet (from sugar, mirin and sake) and citrus (from yuzu and dai dai fruits). Shiso leaves and sansho provide an extra aromatic touch. These flavourings are used over and over again in different combinations. Pickles are carefully chosen to go with particular dishes. Fish and seafood, as befits a nation of islands, play a large part in the cuisine, from the basic soup stock to fishcakes and sausages. An extenstion of this love of seafood has been the use of seaweeds or sea–vegetables, a hallmark of Japanese cooking.

Many of the unique aspects of Japanese cuisine come from the fact that it developed to a great extent in isolation. However, over centuries, a number of foreign influences filtered through. China, between the sixth and eighth centuries, had an effect on many aspects of Japanese life including food – hence chopsticks, tea, the nutritious soya bean, rice and noodles. Zen Buddhism provided both the aesthetic criteria of Japanese cuisine and the emphasis on vegetables. It was only in the nineteenth century that the Japanese began eating red meat more widely. Certain dishes can be traced directly to outside sources, although most have been refined into something quintessentially Japanese. Portugese missionaries in the sixteenth century are said to have requested gambas fritta, fried prawns. From this developed the dish tempura: whole prawns and slices of vegetables cooked briefly in an exquisitely light batter so that the flavour and freshness of the ingredient is highlighted rather than disguised.

JAPANESE LONDON

GLOSSARY

Agar agar (kanten): a vegetarian setting agent obtained from seaweed, available either in powdered form or in translucent strands.

Azuki Beans: small dark red beans. In a sweetened paste form (an), they form a principal ingredient in Japanese cakes.

Bean curd (tofu): an ivory-coloured soy bean product with a firm custard texture, available either fresh or vacuum-packed. Kinu or silk tofu has a more delicate texture than momen or cotton tofu. Koyadofu is freeze-dried tofu, dull brown with a spongy texture. Aburage are thin deep-fried sheets of bean curd.

Bonito: dried bonito flakes, together with kombu seaweed, are used to make dashi soup stock and also as a garnish. Dashi-no-moto is an instant granule form of dashi stock, available in packets.

Burdock (gobo): a long slender root vegetable, available fresh and canned.

Chrysanthemum leaves (shungiku): the leaves of the edible garland chrysanthemum (not to be confused with our ornamental inedible one), used as a garnish and a vegetable.

Daikon: a large, long, mild, white radish, also called mooli in greengrocers. Dried daikon strips, called kiriboshi daikon, need soaking before use.

Fish and Seafood: raw fish, either in sashimi or sushi, is one of the most famous elements of Japanese cuisine. Popular fish include mackerel (saba), salmon (sake) and tuna (maguro), with the latter graded according to its fattiness. Grilled eel (unagi) is a prized delicacy. Popular seafood includes abalone (awabi), horse clams (mirugai), scallops (hotategai), salmon roe (ikura), octopus (tako) and squid (ika).

Fishcakes and fish sausages: boiled, baked and deep-fried fishcakes and sausages come in various forms, and are often found in the deep freeze section. Popular varieties include: naruto maki, a fish sausage with a spiral pink or yellow pattern running through it; satsuma-age, oval-shaped fried fishcake; and chukuwu, a fish sausage.

Flours: rice flour (joshinko) is used for savoury doughs. Glutinous rice flour (mochiko) and soya bean flour (kinako) are used mainly for desserts.

Gingko nuts (ginnan): maidenhair tree kernels. Fresh gingko nuts (which need shelling) are ivory-cloured, while tinned, shelled gingko nuts are pale green.

Kabocha: Japanese pumpkin, often sold deep-frozen.

Kampyo: dried gourd or winter melon strips, used for tying food.

Kinome: prickly ash tree leaf, used as a garnish.

Konnyaku: a bland, glutinous substance made from the root of the devil's tongue plant, often labelled 'alimentary paste' and found in the chilled section or freezer. Konnyaku noodles, called shirataki (meaning white waterfall), are sold packaged in water.

Kuzu: a white starch made from the kuzu vine root, sometimes labelled 'kuzu arrowroot'.

Lotus root (renkon): a crunchy root with a decorative tracery of holes, available fresh, in sausage-like links, or tinned.

Mirin: a sweet Japanese rice wine, used as a glazing ingredient.

Miso: fermented soya bean paste, available in a variety of colours and flavours. It is usually found in the chilled or freezer section and should be stored in the fridge.

Mochi: cooked glutinous rice, pounded to a paste.

Mountain yam (yama no imo): a large, pale-skinned, sweet-flavoured tuber, which comes in different shapes.

Mushrooms: these include large, brown-capped shitake (available both fresh and dried), tiny white-capped clusters of enokidake, light brown shimeji and large, brown matsutake.

Natto: fermented soya beans with a pungent smell and sticky texture.

Noodles: harusame, fine cellophane noodles made from mung beans whose Japanese name means 'spring rain'; soba, brown buckwheat noodles; somen: fine wheatflour noodles, sometimes flavoured with green tea; udon: thick, white wheatflour noodles.

Pickles: sudori shoga, pickled ginger, traditionally eaten with sushi; takuan, pickled daikon, often bright yellow in colour.

Ponzu: a citric vinegar.

Potato starch (kataturika): strongly-binding sweet potato starch.

Rice: short grain, slightly glutinous rice is the staple. A very sticky glutinous 'sweet rice' is used to make desserts and cakes.

Rice vinegar (su): delicate rice vinegar, used in making sushi.

Sake: rice wine, both drunk and used as a flavouring in cooking.

Sansho: known as 'Japanese pepper' this is the seed of the prickly ash tree.

Seaweeds: kombu, a dark large-leafed seaweed used in making dashi stock; nori, thin green sheets of dried seaweed used for sushi, available untoasted or toasted; wakame, dried lobeleaf seaweed.

Shichimi togarashi: a piquant seven-spice mix containing chilli.

Shiso: the aromatic red or green leaves of the perilla or beefsteak plant, used to add both flavour and colour.

Soya beans: raw soya beans (edaname), available frozen, are a snack food. Dried soya beans (daizu) need long cooking.

Soy sauce (shoyu): Japanese soy sauce, available both dark and light, has a different flavour from Chinese soy sauce. Kikkoman is a reputable shoyu manufacturer.

Trefoil (mitsuba): a leaf herb, often found freeze-dried.

Umeboshi: small, deep red, pickled plums, with a tart flavour.

Warabi: young edible sprouts of bracken, picked before they have uncurled, available dried or vacuum-packed.

Wasabi: a pungent green root, compared to horseradish, sold in paste or powder form.

Wheat Gluten (fu): wheat gluten forms, often coloured, used rather like croutons in soups and simmered dishes.

Yuzu: an aromatic citrus fruit, used to flavour oil.

JAPANESE LONDON

FOODSHOPS

Japanese food shops, aimed at the expat business community, demand high prices at which the Japanese themselves grumble. Many of the foodstuffs are imported from Japan and all of these are beautifully packaged, from rice-paper packets of ribbon-wrapped noodles to gaudy, whacky packets of sweets, shaped like robots or calculators. Fish and meat counters are a beautiful sight, with finely-sliced meat and aesthetic arrangements of seafood, from a gracefully-coiled octopus tendril to a mosaic of mackeral fillets.

In general Japanese food shops are well ordered, with ingredients grouped together: flavourings, pickles, noodles. Often, the goods have small labels giving the English names.

CENTRAL

Arigato
48-50 Brewer Street, W1
(020-7-287 1722)
Tube: Leicester Square or Piccadilly Circus
Open: Mon-Sat 10am-9pm; Sun 11am-8pm
Neat and airy, this friendly supermarket-cum-take-away caters for Japanese office workers in the area. The stock covers basics from miso paste to soba noodles. Especially popular is the take-away sushi counter.

Minamoto Kitchoan
44 Piccadilly, W1
(020-7-437 3135)
Tube: Piccadilly Circus
Open: Mon-Fri & Sun 10am-7pm;
Sat 10am-8pm
This dainty shop specialises in Japanese confectionary: exquisite-looking concoctions made from red bean paste, rice flour and fruit and bean jelly, tastefully wrapped and packaged. Prices are high, reflecting the fact that these are traditionally

given as gifts. There is a small seating area where you can sit and enjoy green tea and a cake, such as their bestselling Tsuya (a soft round pancake filled with red bean paste).

Natural House
Japan Centre, 212 Piccadilly, W1
(020-7-434 4218)
Tube: Piccadilly Circus
Open: Mon-Sat 11am-7.30pm; Sun 10am-6pm
Tucked away in the Japan Centre's basement is this well-stocked, busy shop. Homesick Japanese stock up with brightly packaged sweets, with names such as 'Kiss Mint' or 'Vessel in the Fog'. More functional foodstuffs are also well-represented, from noodles to pickled plums and miso, and there are freezers crammed full with seafood and fish cakes and sukiyaki beef. A deli-counter offers take-away snacks.

NORTH

Atari-Ya Foods
595 High Road, N12
(020-8-446 6669)
Tube: West Finchley
Bus: 263
Open: Tue-Fri 10am-6.30pm;
Sat-Sun 10am-7pm
A neat shop dominated by a long fish counter, with the staff behind it expertly preparing the fish. In addition, there is a limited selection of groceries and a small chilled cabinet containing essentials such as fresh tofu.

Wing Yip (London) Ltd
395 Edgware Road, NW2
(020-8-450 0422)
Tube: Colindale
Open: Mon-Sat 9.30am-7pm;
Sun 11.30am-5.30pm
This massive Oriental supermarket, located just off Staples Corner, contains basic bottled and tinned Japanese ingredients: noodles, sauces, tea and sake.

Supermaz Ltd
Oriental City
399 Edgware Road, NW9
(020-8-200 0009)
Tube: Colindale
Open: Mon-Sat 10am-8pm; Sun 12 noon-6pm
Located in the shopping centre formerly known as Yaohan Plaza (which comes complete with a SegaDome and a large Japanese bookshop), this is London's largest Japanese supermarket. Brightly spic and span, the store is clearly laid out and goods are well labelled in English. There is an excellent array of fresh produce, from burdock and lotus root to clusters of tiny enokidake mushrooms, and a fresh fish counter. Stock is comprehensive: from the aisles of noodles, teas, and condiments to the chilled counters with their neatly-packaged fresh fish and meat.

JAPANESE LONDON

EATING PLACES

O nce Japanese restaurants in London were exclusive, elitist, expensive affairs. Two recent trends – the noodle bar and conveyor-belt sushi restaurant – mean that affordable, accessible Japanese food is now widely available.

CENTRAL

Ginnan £££
1-2 Roseberry Court
36a Roseberry Avenue, EC1
(020-7-278 0008)
Tube: Farringdon
Discreet and sedate, this civilized eaterie serves up spanking fresh sushi, tasty noodles and feather-light tempura to a predominantly Japanese clientele.

Hamine £££
84 Brewer Street, W1
(020-7-439 0785)
Tube: Piccadilly Circus
Noodles, whether in a steaming bowl of tasty soup stock or in a cold, garnished noodle salad, are the name of the game here at this down-to-earth popular eating house.

Ikkyu £££
67 Tottenham Court Road, W1
(020-7-636 9280)
Tube: Goodge Street
Hidden in a basement, this relaxed restaurant continues to be popular. Sushi is freshly prepared behind a counter while the set lunch menu includes bargains such as miso ramen, a huge bowl of garnished noodles in a flavourful stock.

Kulu Kulu £££
76 Brewer Street, W1
(020-7-734 7316)
Tube: Piccadilly Circus
A classic example of a kaiten (revolving) sushi bar where diners browse on sushi plucked from a slowly-moving conveyor-belt. The strength here is the quality of the fresh, handmade sushi.

Satsuma £££
56 Wardour Street, W1
(020-7-437 8338)
Tube: Leicester Square or Piccadilly Circus
From the Wagamama School of Refectory-style dining: a sleek, streamlined affair with long wooden tables and benches. Staff are lively and the food, ranging from chicken Teriyaki to sushi, well-presented and tasty.

Ten Ten Tei
56 Brewer Street, W1
020-7-287 1738
Tube: Piccadilly Circus
Tucked away from the hustle of Piccadilly, this friendly, relaxed restaurant serves up good value Japanese food with all the classics on offer, from sashimi to tempura.

Yo! Sushi! £££
52-53 Poland Place, W1
(020-7-287 0443)
Tube: Oxford Circus
Bright and buzzy high-tec restaurant, offering robotic drinks trolleys and conveyor-belt sushi in a frenetic atmosphere.

EAST

Moshi Moshi Sushi £££
Unit 24, Liverpool Street Station, EC2
(020-7-247 3227)
Tube: Liverpool Street
Situated in the bustling station this smart sushi bar serves reasonably-priced, freshly-made sushi on a conveyor-belt system. Punters, including besuited Japanese and European businessmen, sit at the counter, picking off passing plates (with coloured plates signifying different price levels).

NORTH

Café Japan £££
626 Finchley Road, NW11
(020-8-455 6584)
Tube: Golders Green
Excellent sushi, sashmi and yakitori dishes
attract a crowd of regulars to this well-
established Japanese restaurant.

Jin Kichi £££
73 Heath Street, NW3
(020-7-794 6158)
Tube: Hampstead
A relaxed restaurant, predominantly a
yakitori bar, offering a range of tastily salty
sweet skewered foods including chicken and
prawns.

Wakaba ££££
122a Finchley Road, NW3
(020-7-722 3854)
Tube: Finchley Road
The elegant facade, a curve of smoked glass,
and the stark interior comply with one's
expectations of Japanese aesthetics. The food
is cooked with flair, including impressively
fresh seafood.

Oriental City Food Court £
Oriental City Plaza
399 Edgware Road, NW9
(020-8-200 0009)
Tube: Colindale
A busy, noisy indoor 'courtyard' dominated
by a huge central TV with CNN news and
the noise of vendors shouting out their
clients' orders, surrounded by a range of
Oriental foodstalls. The fresh sushi from the
sushi bar next to the supermarket is
particularly good.

WEST

Momo £££
14 Queen's Parade, W5
(020-8-997 0206)
Tube: North Ealing
With the Japanese School close by, this
pleasant restaurant caters for the local
Japanese community and offers deliciously
authentic food at reasonable prices.

Sushi-Hiro ££
1 Station Parade
Uxbridge Road, W5
(020-8-896 3175)
Tube: Ealing Common
Handily situated just across the road from
the tube station is this spic and span sushi
restaurant, discreetly hidden behind a frosted
glass facade, which offers excellent value
sushi to eat in or take-away.

COOKBOOKS

Food of Japan
Shirley Booth
A facinating look at the history of Japanese
cuisine plus tempting recipes.

The Heart of Zen Cookery
Soei Yoneda
An exploration of the centuries-old
vegetarian cuisine of the Zen temples.

Japanese Cookery
Elizabeth Lambert Ortiz
A clearly-written cookbook; a useful intro-
duction to the cuisine.

Way of the Noodle
Russel Cronin
A cultish, entertaining insight into the
Wagamama noodle bar's ethos.

Step-by-Step Japanese Cooking
Leslie Downer and Minoru Yoneda
A clear introduction to Japanese cuisine.

JAPANESE LONDON

95

JEWISH LONDON

The Jewish presence in England dates back to the eleventh century when French Jews followed William the Conqueror and settled here. They were legally restricted to certain trades and professions but moneylending, forbidden to Christians, was allowed, indeed encouraged, and became the basis for a prosperous and established community. Persecution of the Jews grew, however, and in 1290 all Jews were expelled from England by Edward I.

Following the expulsion of Jews from Spain in 1492, some Sephardi Jews (Mediterranean Jews) accepted the Christian faith but continued to practise Judaism in secret. They became known as Marranos and a small community of them settled in London. In 1655 Rabbi Menassah ben Israel, resident in Holland, appealed to Oliver Cromwell to permit Jewish resettlement. In June of the following year Cromwell declared that Judaism would again be permitted in England and a small community of Sephardi merchants, bankers, bullion dealers and gem importers settled in London. The Sephardi community's first synagogue was in a house at Creechurch Lane in the East End. In 1701, when this had become too small, the Bevis Marks synagogue was built – and continues in use to this day.

The Jewish community was also expanded by the immigration of Ashkenazi Jews from Eastern Europe, who followed a different liturgy. In general they were artisans, peasants, tailors and shoemakers. By 1690, they had established their own synagogue in Dukes Place.

George I encouraged German Jews to come to England and by the middle of the eighteenth century the Ashkenazi community outnumbered the Sephardi.

Aldgate and Houndsditch were popular Jewish areas, although in the first half of the nineteenth century a move took place among the established and prosperous Jewish families, such as the Rothschilds and Montefiores, who left St Swithins Lane for the fashionable West End. In 1858, a special parliamentary resolution enabled Lionel de Rothschild to take his seat in the House of Commons, which marked a watershed in Jewish emancipation in Britain. During the late nineteenth century middle-class Jews moved into the new suburbs and by 1882, the St John's Wood synagogue was in operation.

For the poorer Jewish immigrants, however, the East End remained the focus. As Stephen Brook puts it in his fascinating book, *The Club*, 'Jews tend to live in enclaves not out of natural gregariousness but because they want to be close to institutions vital to the life of the community. Religious Jews will not ride or drive on the Sabbath so they wish to live within easy walking distance of a synagogue. They also needed convenient access to Jewish schools (there were seven in existence in 1851) and kosher butchers. Naturally new arrivals tended to join fellow Jews in the areas favoured by those who had arrived before them '

Following the assassination of the liberal Russian Tsar Alexander II in 1881, a series of pogroms was unleashed in Russia and Poland, which continued into the early twentieth century. Thousands of Jews fled westwards, many aiming for and reaching America, but some coming to Britain instead of continuing their journey. Between 1881 and 1914 the Jewish population of the East End swelled by well over 100,000 people. These were Orthodox, Yiddish-speaking, semi-skilled or unskilled Jews; and the already established Anglo-Jews felt ambivalent about the influx, fearing an anti-Semitic backlash.

The Ashkenazi immigrants moved into the East End, especially around Whitechapel. Foodshops sold the herrings and pickles of their homelands and the number of chevras (small synagogues) grew. The United Synagogues established dispersal committees to encourage Jewish immigrants to move out of the East End into the expanding suburbs of Dalston, Stoke Newington and Hackney. In the 1920s there was a move northwards from the East End into Stamford Hill and then into the newly established suburbs of Golders Green, Edgware and Ilford. The rise of anti-Semitism in the 1930s brought in around 70,000 Jews from Central Europe, with the influx increasing sharply after the 1938 Anschluss (unification) with Austria and the Kristallnacht pogrom. These were prosperous middle-class refugees who settled in north-west London in areas such as Hampstead, St John's Wood and Swiss Cottage. The decline of the Jewish East End community was hastened by the war. Bombing destroyed both families and property. Instead of returning after service or evacuation, many East End Jews opted for the suburbs with their by now well-established Jewish communities. By the 1970s the population of the East End Jewish community had shrunk to less than 5,000; today, around a third of Britain's Jewish population lives in north-west London.

JEWISH CUISINE

Jewish cuisine reflects the widely-dispersed Jewish community by containing a range of dishes and styles of cooking from around the world. Two broad and diverse strands stem from the culinary traditions of the Ashkenazi and the Sephardi. The former, influenced by long, cold winters, features preserved and pickled dishes such as rollmop herrings and smoked salmon; while the latter delights in aromatic spices and Mediterranean produce such as aubergines, peppers and olive oil. Common to all Jewish food, however, are the Kashrut, the strict dietary laws governing the preparation and consumption of food, which stem from biblical injunctions. They have been adhered to over the centuries.

Leviticus permits certain fish and meat: 'Any animal that has true hoofs, with clefts through the hoofs, and that chews the cud such you may eat' and 'Anything in water, whether in the seas or in the streams, that has fins and scales these you may eat'. Cattle, sheep and most fish, therefore, are permitted, but pigs, rabbits and shellfish are not, neither certain birds nor anything that crawls or swarms. Permitted animals and birds must be ritually slaughtered in a way that allows as much blood as possible to drain from the carcass. As the consumption of blood is forbidden, raw meat must be 'koshered' by being soaked in water, treated with salt, drained and then rinsed.

The injunction 'Thou shalt not boil a kid in its mother's milk' has been interpreted to mean that meat and dairy products may not be consumed together. Food containing dairy products may not be eaten after meat until at least three hours have passed. This extends to separating kitchen equipment used for meat products from that for dairy products. 'Pareve' means neutral and refers to foods that may be eaten with either meat or dairy products.

The commandment that 'On the seventh day thou shalt do no work, neither thy maidservant nor thy manservant' has produced a range of characteristically Jewish dishes that are prepared the day before they are eaten. Cholent is one of the most famous of these dishes: a Sabbath stew traditionally cooked slowly overnight. Harry Blacker, in his book of East End reminiscences *Just Like It Was*, writes of the cholent being 'carried to the nearest bakehouse, where for a small consideration (about 2 pence), the baker would put the pan in the oven to cook until the following midday'.

Religious festivals also influence Jewish cuisine. At Pesach (Passover), when wheat flour is banned, dishes are made with ground nuts, matzo meal or potato flour. Certain symbolic foods and dishes are eaten both during the weekly Shabbat (Sabbath) and the festivals. During Pesach, which celebrates the Jewish delivery from slavery to the Egyptians, a 'Seder' plate is assembled made up of symbolic ingredients such as haroset, a sweet fruit paste representing the mortar used by Jewish slaves when they worked on the Pharoah's cities, and a bitter herb, such as endive, representing the bitterness endured during slavery. Matzos, the unleavened bread used during Pesach, represents the bread which didn't have time to rise as the Jews fled.

Another element common to Jewish cookery across the continents is its ingenuity, born out of the poverty and lack of ingredients which Jewish communities often suffered. Meat, in particular, was eked out in resouceful dishes such as helzel, stuffed chicken neck skin, and koureven, stewed chicken gizzards.

GLOSSARY

Bagels: circular bread rolls with a distinctive, chewy texture which comes from being first boiled then baked. Increasingly available both plain and flavoured.

Bulka: the 'everyday' cholla loaf, made from the same dough as bagels but shaped differently.

Cholla: a symbolic plaited loaf made from an egg-rich dough, and with a brown glaze. It plays a prominent part in most Jewish festivals and is especially associated with Shabbat, the weekly Sabbath.

Chopped liver: a tasty mixture of finely-chopped liver, onion and hard-boiled egg.

Falafel: small, savoury chick-pea croquettes, now regarded as an Israeli national dish.

Gefilte fish: minced fish balls, either poached or fried.

Herrings: a staple fish, preserved by salting or pickling. Chopped herring: a sweet-sour

mixture of herrings, onions, apple, sugar and vinegar; rollmops or Bismarcks, pickled herrings rolled round onion rings; schmaltz herrings or matjes: smoked young herrings, often ready-filleted.

Kreplach: triangular dumplings with a meat or cheese filling. The three corners symbolise the three patriarchs: Abraham, Isaac and Jacob. These can be found ready-made in freezer sections.

Latkes: shredded potato fritters associated with Chanucah.

Lokshen: egg noodles, used in soups and also to make lokshen kugel, a rich baked pudding, traditionally baked overnight for Shabbat.

Mandlen: from Yiddish for 'almonds', these are fried or baked dough 'soup nuts', used like croutons as a garnish.

Matzos: a flat unleavened bread, similar in texture and taste to a water biscuit. It is the main element in Passover cookery, which forbids the use of leavened grain. The entire process of matzo-making must take no longer than 18 minutes, otherwise fermentation may start.

Matzo balls (knaidlach): walnut-sized, matzo-meal dumplings.

Matzo meal: a binding element made from finely ground matzos.

Rye bread: bread made from rye, with a distinctively rich flavour.

Salt beef: boiled and pickled beef, usually brisket. Available freshly-made or in packets.

Smoked salmon (lox): traditionally served in a fresh bagel with cream cheese. Available pre-sliced or freshly sliced.

JEWISH LONDON

FOODSHOPS

T he food shop has always been important in Jewish life, both to satisfy religious dietary needs and as a focus of identification. The food that we find in Jewish shops in Britain is predominantly Ashkenazi rather than Sephardi. In *East End Story*, A. B. Levy remembers the aromas that 'wafted through the open fronts of delicatessen shops, from smoked salmon and roe, barrelled cucumbers and sauerkraut, and herrings in various guises, kippered, schmaltz, chopped and pickled.' These items continue to be familiar Jewish deli fare but nearly all the East End shops have gone and the delicatessens are now found in the North-London suburbs.

Perhaps what is most baffling for a non-Jew are the varying degrees of kosherness. The Kashrut are strict dietery laws which govern the preparation and consumption of foods. Certain food shops display certificates to show that they are supervised or licensed by authorities such as the Kedassia, the Joint Kashrus Committee of the Union of Orthodox Hebrew Congregations, the Adam Yisroel Synagogue and the Golders Green Beth Hamedrash Congregation. These are the shops and eating places that I have called 'kosher' in my guide, but readers should satisfy themselves as to the standards of Kashrut observed. Some shops have a large range of kosher foodstuffs without being supervised while others carry a range of non-kosher Jewish foods. Interest in kosher food is reviving among younger Jews and the shops are responding to this. Kosher food, nowadays, is an increasingly sophisticated business and the range of kosher items available has increased enormously, from tandoori chicken to champagne.

JEWISH LONDON

J.Rogg Delicatessen

EAST

Brick Lane Beigel Bake

159 Brick Lane, E1
(020-7-729 0616)
Tube: Liverpool Street
Open: Daily 24 hours
This small, reasonably-priced bakery, piled high with bagels and chollas, is enormously popular. A trip to Brick Lane market on a Sunday simply wouldn't be complete without one of their bagels – a fact confirmed by the perpetual, straggling queue.

Ilford Kosher Meats

7 Beehive Lane
Ilford, IG4
(020-8-554 3238)
Tube: Gants Hill
Open: Mon 6.30am-5pm;
Tue-Thur 6.30am-6pm;
Fri 6.30am-1pm; Sun 7am-1pm
This large butcher's shop, run with genuine enthusiasm by Mr Morris Brown, has an excellent selection of kosher meat products. Everything is made on the premises, from the lamb and mint sausages to the de-boned stuffed chicken. Traditional dishes include helzel (chicken neck stuffing) and, a family speciality, Russian Verrainitz: pastry-wrapped mashed potato, liver and onion from an old recipe handed down by Mr Brown's grandmother.

Ridley Bagel Bakery

13-15 Ridley Road, E8
(020-7-923 0666)
BR: Dalston Kingsland
Open: Daily 24 hours
This down-to-earth shop offers Jamaican patties side-by-side with bagels and chollas and attracts a steady stream of hungry customers.

J. Rogg Delicatessen

137 Cannon Street Road, E1
(020-7-488 3368)
Tube: Aldgate East, Whitechapel or Shadwell
Open: Mon-Fri 9am-5.30pm;
Sun 7am-2.30pm
This delightful corner shop is an East End institution. Barry started working in it in 1946 when he was 16 and customers returning after decades away testify that the shop still looks the same. Pyramids of Krakus pickle tins line the shelves and sausages dangle down, while in a number of tubs lie Barry's famous homemade new green pickles, flavoured with garlic, bay leaves and chillies. His schmaltz herrings are also feted, along with the homemade salt beef, chopped liver, freshly-fried fish, gefilte fish balls and chopped herring. Barry himself, on first-name terms with most of his customers, is an attraction – a genial figure still holding on to a unique way of life.

NORTH

Amazing Grapes

94 Brent Street, NW4
(020-8-202 2631)
Tube: Hendon Central
Open: Mon–Wed 9am-6pm; Thur 9am-7pm;
Fri 9am-6pm in summertime (1¹/₂ hours before Shabbat in winter); Sun 10am-2pm
This well-stocked kosher off-licence sells kosher wines from all over the world, reflecting the increasing range available. They stock Kiddush, the strong, sweet red wine used for sacramental purposes, and Israeli wines.

La Boucherie (Kosher) Ltd

4 Cat Hill
East Barnet, EN4
(020-8-449 9215)
Tube: Cockfosters
Open: Mon 8.30am-2.30pm;
Tue–Thur 8.30am-5pm; Fri 8am-1pm;
Sun 8.30am-1.30pm & 3.30pm-7.30pm

This vast, sleek, scrupulously-clean shop is one of the leading kosher butchers and consequently bustles with customers. There are 40 staff altogether, including six chefs working behind the scenes on ready-made dishes such as Boeuf Wellington and the kofte kebabs for which La Boucherie is famous.

Carmelli Bakeries

128 Golders Green Road, NW11
(020-8-455 3063)
Tube: Golders Green
Open: Mon-Wed 7am-1am;
Thur all night; Fri 7am-2pm;
Sat all night, through to Sun 11pm
Smart and glitzy, this famous kosher bakery continues to attract crowds of customers. Noted for its bagels, it also offers a host of breads, cakes, pastries, quiches and biscuits. It is divided into a Parev or 'non-milky' counter and a 'milky' counter, while behind-scenes bustles with bakers producing the goods.

J. A. Corney Ltd

9 Hallswelle Parade
Finchley Road, NW11
(020-8-455 9588)
Tube: Golders Green
Open: Tue-Thur 7.30am-5pm;
Fri 7.30am-4pm; Sat & Sun 7.30am-1pm
This well-established fishmonger's has been in the Corney family for over 30 years. It stocks a large range of fish, such St Peter's fish and carp, plus minced fish (a mix of haddock, whiting and bream) – with more expensive fish minced on demand. Staff are friendly and knowledgeable.

Country Market Ltd

136 Golders Green Road, NW11
(020-8–455 3289)
Tube: Golders Green
Open: Mon–Sat 8am–10pm; Sun 10am-4pm
A large store with a deli-counter and fresh fish section, plus frozen kosher dishes and Osem and Kelmans kosher groceries.

Daniel's Bagel Bakery

13 Halleswelle Parade
Finchley Road, NW11
(020-8-455 5826)
Tube: Golders Green
Open: Sun-Wed 7am-9pm; Thur 7am-10pm;
Fri 7am-1$1/_2$ hours before Shabbat
A kosher bakery noted for its excellent bagels as well as a good range of cholla, rye bread and pastries.

Hendon Bagel Deli

35-7 Church Road, NW4
(020-8-203 6919)
Tube: Hendon Central
Open: Mon-Thur 7am-11pm;
Fri 8am-3pm; Sat open 7pm-Sun 11pm
A well-established and popular kosher bakery, selling bulka, dark and light rye breads and a wide range of bagels. On Thursdays and Fridays, piles of freshly baked chollas lie temptingly on the racks.

L & D Foods Ltd

17 Lyttleton Road, N2
(020-8-455 8397)
Bus: 102
Open: Mon, Wed & Thur 8.30am-5.30pm;
Tue 8.30am-1pm; Fri 7am-4pm;
Sun 7am-1pm
This established family business has been selling top-notch delicacies and providing a delivery service to customers in north-west London and the West End for over 30 years. The store's speciality is its superb smoked salmon, freshly hand-sliced and sent all over the world. The comprehensive stock includes more unusual items, with a strong emphasis on quality.

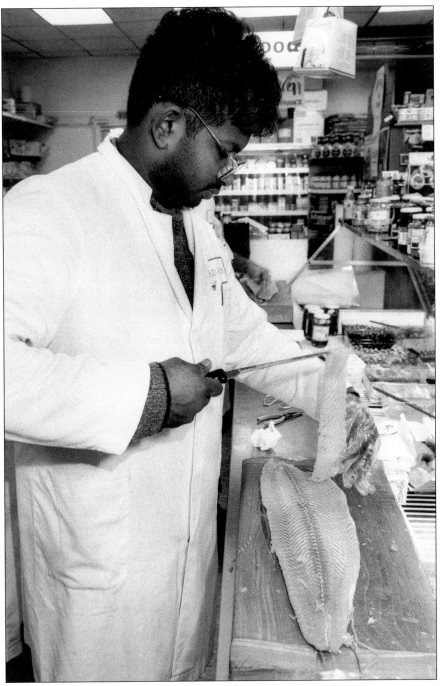

L&D Food

Louis Mann and Son Ltd
23 Edgwarebury Lane, WD6
(020-8-958 4910)
Tube: Edgware
Open: Mon 8am-1pm; Tue-Thur 8am-5pm;
Fri 8am-1pm, Sun 8am-1pm
A smart, well-established kosher butcher,
run with friendly efficiency by the Mann
family. Salt beef, sold hot on Sundays, and
hot roast chickens, sold daily, are especially
popular.

Panzer's
13-19 Circus Road, NW8
(020-7-722 8162/8596)
Tube: St John's Wood
Open: Mon-Fri 8am-7pm;
Sat 8am-6pm; Sun 9am-2pm
Warmly recommended by Evelyn Rose, the
doyenne of Jewish cookery, this large
bustling delicatessen has been established
since 1955, with Peter Vogel carrying on the
family tradition. In its range and depth of
stock, Panzer's is more like a supermarket
than a deli, stocking everything from
Hershey chocolate bars (for the area's ex-pat
American community) to Israeli wine.
Although not supervised, there is a large
selection of kosher lines plus traditional
Jewish foodstuffs. The large deli-counter
offers six types of herring and four grades of
smoked salmon among its delicacies, and its
smoked salmon bagels are a must for
afficionados.

Raoul's Deli
394 Uxbridge Road
Hatch End
(020-8-428 4929)
Tube: Pinner
Open: Mon 8.30am-1pm;
Tue-Thur 8.30am-5.30pm;
Fri 8am-2pm; Sun 8am-1.30pm
This attractive kosher delicatessen has a small
bakery counter selling freshly-made bagels,
pastries and biscuits; a long deli counter and
a large freezer section.

Ridley Bagel Bakery
105 High Road, N2
(020-8-442 0019)
Tube: East Finchley
Open: Mon-Sat 8am-5pm; Sun 8am-3pm
A friendly branch of the famous Dalston
bakery, offering a selection of bagels, breads
and cakes plus a small deli counter.

Ivor Silverman
4 Canons Corner
London Road, Stanmore
(020-8-958 8682/2692)
Tube: Stanmore
Open: Mon 8am-1pm;
Tue-Thur 8am-5.30pm;
Fri 8am-1pm; Sun 8am-1pm
An elegant and upmarket kosher butcher's
which, in addition to freshly-cut meat and
poultry, offers a large range of prepared
meat dishes.

Steve's Kosher Kitchen
5 Canons Corner
London Road, Stanmore
(020-8-958 9446)
Tube: Stanmore
Open: Mon 8.30am-1.30pm; Tue-Thur
8.30am-5.30pm; Fri 8am-1pm; Sun 8am-1pm
A kosher delicatessen with an excellent
selection of homemade foods. Specialities
include chopped liver, salt beef and shallow-
fried fish 'like granny used to do'.

Sam Stoller and Son
28 Temple Fortune Parade, NW11
(020-8-458 1429)
Tube: Golders Green
Open: Mon 8am-1pm, Tue-Thur 7am-5pm;
Fri 7am-1 hour before Shabbat; Sun 8am-1pm
Mr Sam Stoller opened his first
fishmonger's in 1932. He took over this
attractive tiled shop in 1947 and is known
as one of the leading kosher fishmonger's.
The smoked salmon is particularly good,
plus the 'prime kosher fish' such as St
Peter's fish and Israeli carp.

JEWISH LONDON

EATING PLACES

CENTRAL

CENTRAL

Reubens £ £
20a Baker Street, W1
(020-7-935 5945)
Tube: Baker Street
A popular, well-established kosher eating
place offering French and Jewish food, from
steak au poivre to chicken soup.

NORTH

Aviv £ £
87 High Street, HA8
(020-8-952 2484)
Tube: Edgware
A well-established kosher restaurant that
specialises in Israeli food, hence there is a
definite Middle-Eastern flavour to the menu
which offers mezze (including excellent
houmous) and grilled meats.

Blooms £ £
130 Golders Green Road, NW11
(020-8-455 1338)
Tube: Golders Green
Opened in 1965, this Golders Green
institution has survived its better-known
Whitechapel counterpart and continues to
offer traditional kosher Jewish food. The salt
beef is famous and portions are generous –
homely food in a vintage atmosphere.

Chit Chat £ £
85 Golders Green Road, NW11
(020-8-731 6255)
Tube: Golders Green
A modern restaurant serving excellent
Mediterranean Jewish foods: lots of the
salads so beloved by Israelis and large
portions of tasty grilled meats.

Taboon £
17 Russell Parade
Golders Green Road, NW11
(020-8-455 7451)
Tube: Golders Green
Taboon does a roaring trade in take-away
falaffel: deliciously juicy, freshly-fried
chickpea rissoles garnished with good salad
and tahini – a world away from the small,
dry balls normally on offer.

COOKBOOKS

**Jewish Cooking from
Around the World**
Josephine Bacon
A lively and accessible cookbook exploring
both Sephardi and Ashkenazi cooking.

The Jewish Holiday Cookbook
Gloria Kaufner Greene
An informative look at festival and holiday
dishes.

The Book of Jewish Food
Claudia Roden
A wonderful exploration of Jewish cookery
around the world.

**The Complete International
Jewish Cookbook**
Evelyn Rose
An excellent basic and reliable cookbook by
the doyenne of Jewish cookery.

New Jewish Cuisine
Evelyn Rose
A straightforward look at Jewish recipes.

JEWISH LONDON

MIDDLE-EASTERN LONDON

Super Bahar

T he Middle-Eastern community in London comprises several different nationalities. Egyptians came to Britain in the 1940s and 1950s both for education and work. The Turkish community is predominantly Turkish-Cypriot – many came to Britain because they were displaced following the Turkish invasion of Cyprus in 1974. They are mainly based in Islington, Hackney and Haringey, with the Stoke Newington end of Green Lanes being a particular focal point. Many of the cafés and kebab houses remain male preserves, with the sound of backgammon being played behind the scenes.

The oil boom in the 1970s and the discovery by Arab countries of new sources of wealth and power meant an increasingly wealthy Arab presence in London, mainly focused around Mayfair and Kensington. A series of political disturbances has also contributed considerably to the Middle-Eastern presence here. The overthrow of the Shah and the Iranian revolution brought in an influx of wealthy Iranian families who were able to use their money and connections to escape, many to America but some to London. They were followed by political opponents of the Ayatollah, seeking refuge. The civil war in Lebanon has resulted in a substantial Lebanese presence in London. Edgware Road, Bayswater, Mayfair, Knightsbridge and Kensington together form the heartland of the Middle-Eastern community, served by its own restaurants, fruit juice bars, cafés, banks, shops and clubs.

MIDDLE-EASTERN CUISINE

T his is an ancient cuisine, in which recipes can be traced back hundreds of years. An Egyptian recipe for melokhia soup, for example, dates from the time of the Pharoahs. The former spice routes which passed through the Middle East have left a fragrant legacy in the region's cooking.

Claudia Roden, an authoritative and knowledgeable writer on Middle-Eastern cookery, identifies four main strands: Iranian or Persian, Arab, Ottoman Turkish and North African. Iranian cuisine is subtle and refined, a product of ancient Persia. Rice forms the heart of the cuisine and is carefullly cooked and exquisitely garnished. The combination of meat with fruit or nuts is a hallmark of the Persian kitchen, shown in dishes such as koresh-e-fesenjan, chicken in walnut and pomegranate sauce. Arab cuisine is very flavourful, using both strong-tasting herbs such as mint and coriander and fragrant spices such as cardamom, cinnamon and allspice. Grilled meats are popular, served with rice, burghul or flat breads.

During the Ottoman Empire, Turkish cuisine reached luxurious heights. Cooking at the Topkapi Palace in Istanbul followed a strict pattern of rules, still followed by chefs today. Ottoman food was spread through the Empire by the army and its followers, with shish kebab said to date back to these warlike days, when Turkish soldiers cooked over their camp fires. This culinary legacy includes numerous stuffed vegetables, such as imam bayaldi (an aubergine dish named after a priest who swooned with delight upon trying it); and layered nutty pastries in sweet syrups, beloved throughout the Middle East. North-African cooking, in contrast to the other cuisines, has a fiery element, produced by hot sauces such as harissa. It is also a cuisine of subtle and delicate spicing.

The influence of Islam means that certain dietary laws are observed throughout the Middle East. Pork is forbidden and meat must be ritually slaughtered and drained of blood. Lamb is the most highly-prized meat throughout the region. Yogurt is widely used: as a refreshing drink, in hot and cold soups, and in salads and marinades.

MIDDLE-EASTERN LONDON

107

GLOSSARY

Allspice: round berry, similar to peppercorns, with a flavour of nutmeg, cinnamon and cloves.

Apricot paste sheets (amretin): translucent orange sheets made from apricots which, when diluted with water, make a refreshing drink. Especially popular during the fasting month of Ramadan.

Arab bread (khoubz): flat round bread

Barberries (zerezhk): tart, red berries, used dried in Iranian cooking to add colour and flavour.

Burghul (bulgar): parboiled, cracked grains of wheat, available both coarse or finely ground.

Coriander: a flat-leafed green herb, similar to continental parsley but with a distinctive sharp taste.

Couscous: fine yellow cereal made from semolina.

Dibbis: thick, dark brown syrup made from dates.

Dill: a caraway-scented herb with fine, feathery green fronds.

Dried limes (limoo): hard, brown, dried limes, used to add a distinctive flavour to Iranian and Iraqi soups and stews.

Filo: paper-thin fine pastry usually found frozen but occasionally available fresh.

Harissa: a fiery, red pimento paste.

Kashk: stony lumps of pungent-smelling dried buttermilk, used in soups and stews. Also available in powdered form.

Konafa (kadaif): a vermicelli-like dough, white in its raw state but resembling shredded wheat once cooked.

Labne (lebne): thick, strained concentrated yogurt (usually sold bottled) which has been shaped into balls, and floats in oil.

Mahlab: small pale brown seeds which are the kernels of blackcherry stones, with a spicy fragrance.

Melokhia: a green, leafy vegetable, similar in appearance to mallow, used in making a famous eponymous Egyptian soup. Fresh melokhia is sometimes found, while dried is readily available.

Merguez: a spicy sausage from North Africa.

Okra: tapering, ridged green pods, available fresh, dried, tinned or frozen.

Onion seeds (sharmar): small, black teardrop-shaped seeds, not related to onions!

Orange–flower water: a fragrant flavouring made from orange flower essence, used in sweets, drinks and desserts.

Orange peel: fine strips of dried orange peel, traditionally from sour (Seville) oranges.

Pine nuts: small, ivory-coloured kernels, with the fine, long Lebanese pine nuts being particularly prized.

Pistachio: a small, green-coloured nut, indigenous to Iran.

Pomegranate syrup: made from the concentrated juice of sour pomegranates and used in Iranian cooking.

Pulses: black-eyed beans, with characteristic black markings; chickpeas, rounded yellow peas; Egyptian brown beans (ful), small brown broad beans.

Quince: a hard yellow-skinned fruit, resembling a large, craggy pear. Usually cooked, whereupon its flesh turns pink.

Rice: long-grain rice is a Middle-Eastern staple. Fine-quality Iranian rice is hard to get over here, with Basmati rice being the closest substitute.

Rose water: an essential scented flavouring made from rose essence and used in sweets and desserts.

Saffron: a costly spice made from the stigmas of a particular crocus variety, sold in thread or powdered form.

Salep: a thickening agent made from dried, crushed orchid roots, used in Iran to thicken ice cream.

Sumac: a dark red powdery spice, made from crushed berries, with a tangy flavour. Sometimes diluted and used as a lemon equivalent.

Tahini: sesame-seed paste.

Tamarind: a brown pod with sour, dark brown, pulpy flesh and seeds. Available in de-seeded pulp form or as a paste. Also used to make a syrup, which is then diluted into a refreshing drink.

Turmeric: an orange-fleshed root, usually sold in its ground form as a yellow-orange powder. It has a harsh, flat taste and is used to add flavour and a distinctive yellow colour to dishes.

Vine leaves: large, distinctively-shaped leaves of the vine. Occasionally found fresh, but more usually sold in packets, preserved in brine, when they require soaking in water.

Yogurt: tangy sheep's and goat's yogurt as well as cow's yogurt is widely used in Middle-Eastern cooking.

Zahtar: a spice mix made from thyme, salt, sumac and sometimes roasted sesame seeds, often baked on the top of breads.

MIDDLE-EASTERN LONDON

FOODSHOPS

A ttractive greengrocer's-cum-delis selling everything from bunches of fresh herbs to pretty pastries, as well as baker's and halal butcher's all serve the Middle-Eastern community in London.

MIDDLE-EASTERN LONDON

CENTRAL

Bustling Edgware Road is filled with Middle-Eastern grocers, cafés and restaurants, and is well worth exploring if you're at all interested in Middle-Eastern food. Drive up it late at night and you'll see a lively, metropolitan scene – with drivers pulling in to get a take-away kebab and people sitting on pavement tables watching the world go by.

Green Valley
36 Upper Berkeley Street, W1
(020-7-402 7385)
Tube: Marble Arch
Open: Mon-Sun 8am-10pm
Warmly recommended by cookery writer Claudia Roden, this smart, roomy Lebanese shop off the Edgware Road is noted for its array of pastries, arranged temptingly in the window. In addition, it keeps an excellent range of foodstuffs: sacks of grains, nuts and pulses and a selection of fresh fruit and vegetables. The finishing touch is the nut counter at the back, with its selection of quality pistachios, almonds and other nuts, plus freshly ground coffee with powdered cardamom added to taste.

EAST

Turkish Food Centre
89 Ridley Road, E8
(020-7-254 6754)
BR: Dalston Junction
Open: Mon-Sat 9am-7.30pm;
Sun 8.30am-7pm
A large, down-to-earth, competitively-priced Turkish supermarket, complete with a halal meat counter selling lamb, mutton and

quails; and a cheese counter and piles of fresh fruits and vegetables – including bunches of leafy greens, vine tomatoes and watermelons. The large bakery section does a roaring trade in kibbeh and loaves of flat 'pide' bread.

NORTH

Yasar Halim
493-495 Green Lanes, N4
020-8-340 8090
Tube: Manor House
Open: Mon 8am-9.30pm; Tue-Sun 8am-10pm
'Haringey's best supermarket!' declares a sign inside this bustling Turkish food shop, which usefully combines a bakery, greengrocer's, deli and halal meat counter. Now in its 18th year, one can find everything at Halim's from fresh green almonds and bunches of truly fresh flat-leaf parsley to jars of quince marmalade. The bakery, however, is the reason (and rightly so) for the shop's popularity. Trays of freshly-baked sweet and savoury pastries are brought into the shop still warm from the oven, while fresh filo and kadaif is also on sale. Staff are both numerous and friendly, and ready to courteously identify the huge array of baked goodies on display.

WEST

Archie Foodstore
14 Moscow Road, W2
(020-7-229 2275)
Tube: Bayswater & Queensway
Open: Mon-Sun 8am-8pm
Next to the Athenian Stores is this well-stocked grocer's, which keeps a wonderful selection of fruit and vegetables such as fresh dates, pomegranates, quinces and kohlrabi.

Badr Butcher's
83 Golborne Road, W10
(020-8-969 5727)
Tube: Ladbroke Grove or Westbourne Park
Open: Mon-Sat 10am-5pm
This small neat shop is dominated by a halal meat counter, offering lamb, chicken and homemade merguez, while the shelves are filled with basic Moroccan stock such as olive oil and couscous.

Crackers
272 Kensington High Street, W8
(020-7-603 7071)
Tube: Kensington High Street
Open: Mon-Fri 9am-8pm, Sat 9.30am-8pm
An attractive delicatessen with predominantly Lebanese stock: pastries, nuts, meats, pulses, grains, spices and syrups plus a range of homemade delicacies. Staff are courteous and helpful.

Le Marrakech
64 Golborne Road, W10
(020-8-964 8307)
Tube: Ladbroke Grove
Open: Mon-Sat 8.30am-7.30pm;
Sun 10am-4pm
An attractive front-of-shop display of earthenware tagines indicates this foodshop's Moroccan roots. Inside, this friendly shop offers delights such as olives with kumquats, pomegranate molasses and pickled lemons, with cookware including couscoussiers and gilded tea-glasses. Lanterns, chandeliers and wall-hangings create something of a bazaar atmosphere – compounded on my visit by one of the staff pulling out a box of Moroccan leather slippers and offering them to an interested punter.

Reza Meat Ltd
347 Kensington High Street, W14
(020-7-603 0924)
Tube: Kensington High Street
Open: Mon-Sun 9am-8pm
A well-arranged Iranian store with a halal butcher's section at the back, groceries and a beautiful selection of fresh fruits, herbs and vegetables outside. Stock includes lumps of kashk (dried yogurt), pickles, labne and a fine range of spices.

Reza Patisserie
345 Kensington High Street, W14
(020-7-602 3674)
Tube: Kensington High Street
Open: Mon-Sun 8.30am-9pm
The wrought-iron table and chairs perched outside this pretty patisserie evoke a leisurely café lifestyle. All the pastries are baked on the premises and are a tempting mixture of Arabic, characterised by nuts and honey, and Iranian, which are simpler and more subtle. The freezer contains Iranian ice creams, flavoured with rose water and saffron, while the shelves hold an array of nuts, sweetmeats and dried fruit, such as Iranian sour cherries.

Super Bahar
349a Kensington High Street, W14
(020-7-603 5083)
Tube: Kensington High Street
Open: Mon-Sun 9am-9pm
This well-stocked Iranian greengrocer's-cum-grocer's is warmly recommended by food writer Margaret Shaida, author of the Glenfiddich Award-winning *The Legendary Cuisine of Persia*. Here she says 'you can find everything you need for Persian cooking'. Outside are tempting piles of fruit, herbs and vegetables such as tiny green grapes and baby okra, while inside the stock is extensive, with much of it labelled in English. The owner is also 'extremely helpful'.

MIDDLE-EASTERN LONDON

111

EATING PLACES

L ondon's thriving Middle-Eastern restaurants cater very much for the ex-pat community and as a result, standards are generally high. The range is such that you can enjoy simple but good street food such as a succulent lamb kebab washed down with fresh fruit juice, or a leisurely meal of sophisticated Lebanese mezze in elegant surroundings.

CENTRAL

Al–Hamra £££target£
31-3 Shepherd Market, W1
(020-7-493 1954)
Tube: Green Park
Elegant surroundings, efficient service and fine Lebanese food combine in one of London's best-known Lebanese restaurants, with prices reflecting the affluent location. The mezze are superb (including delights such as walnut-stuffed baby aubergines) but the atmosphere and service can be on the chilly side.

Ali Baba ££
32 Ivor Place, NW1
(020-7-723 5805)
Tube: Baker Street
This small, unpretentious restaurant is recommended by Claudia Roden for its Egyptian food which as she says is both 'good' and 'very cheap'.

Efes Kebab House ££
80 Great Titchfield Street, W1
(020-7-636 1953)
Tube: Great Portland Street or Oxford Circus
This enormous Turkish restaurant – very much an institution – continues to run with smooth efficiency. The menu caters for carnivores, with charcoal-grilled kebabs much in evidence.

Iran the Restaurant ££££
59 Edgware Road, W2
(020-7-723 1344)
Tube: Edgware Road
A chance to enjoy top-notch Persian cooking – such as rich Chicken Fesanjoon (in a walnut sauce) and deliciously moreish flat Persian bread freshly-baked in the huge clay oven – in wonderfully glitzy surroundings.

Maroush ££££
21 Edgware Road, W2
(020-7-723 0773/262 1090)
Tube: Marble Arch
Very much an Edgware Road institution, this smart Lebanese restaurant serves up high-quality food, complete with live entertainment at weekends.

Meshwar £££
128 Edgware Road, W2
(020-7-262 8304)
Tube: Marble Arch
At the front, the take-away section (frequented predominantly by besuited Lebanese men) serves excellent lamb and chicken kebabs. The back room offers the chance to try some tasty Lebanese food, courteously served in pleasant surroundings.

Ranoush Juice Bar £
43 Edgware Road, W2
(020-7-723 5929)
Tube: Marble Arch
Gleamingly glitzy with its black marble interior, this take-away bar serves up fresh fruit juices and tasty Lebanese snacks with panache.

EAST

Anatolya £
263a Mare Street, E8
(020-8-986 2223)
BR: Hackney Central
A friendly down-to-earth Turkish caff,
serving generous portions of gutsy food.

Mangal £
10 Arcola Street, E8
(020-7-275 8981)
BR: Dalston Kingsland
A famous Stoke Newington eaterie offering
tasty charcoal-grilled kebabs.
Also at: 4 Stoke Newington Road, N16

NORTH-WEST

Hafez ££
559 Finchley Road, NW3
(020-7-431 4546)
Tube: Finchley Road
Recommended by Iranian friends for its
authentic food, this is the slightly more
glitzy sister restaurant of the Hereford Road
branch in West London. Sunday lunchtime
here is a social event.

Laurent ££
428 Finchley Road, NW2
(020-7-794 3603)
Bus: 13
A homely, unpretentious restaurant serving
just couscous, in five different ways.
Portions are generous and standards high.

WEST

Adams Cafe ££
77 Askew Road, W12
(020-8-743 0572)
Bus: 12, 207 or 266
Although the fame of this relaxed restaurant
has spread, it continues to offer delicious
Tunisian food at reasonable prices. The
couscous is a house speciality.

Alounak £
10 Russell Gardens, W14
(020-7-603 7645)
Tube: Olympia
Originally housed in a portacabin in an
Olympia car park, Alounak has expanded
into more conventional premises. Still on
offer, however, is gutsy Persian food –
excellent lamb kebabs and flavourful stews.
Also at: 44 Westbourne Grove, W2
(020-7-229 0416)

Hafez ££
5 Hereford Road, W2
(020-7-221 3167/229 9398)
Tube: Bayswater,
Notting Hill Gate or Queensway
A relaxed and lively Iranian restaurant,
noted for its good food and recommended
by foodwriter Margaret Shaida.

Phoenicia £££
11-13 Abingdon Road, W8
(020-7-937 0120)
Tube: High Street Kensington
An attractive Lebanese restaurant, with
courtous service. Mezze are an effective way
in which to sample a range of Lebanese hors
d'oeuvres, such as labneh and aubergine dip.

COOKBOOKS

The Legendary Cuisine of Persia
Margaret Shaida
An elegantly-written, knowledgeable book
charting the history of Persian cuisine and
filled with excellent recipes.

The New Book of
Middle Eastern Food
Claudia Roden
An invaluable and classic book on Middle-
Eastern cookery, evocatively and
authoritatively written, with tempting recipes.

MIDDLE-EASTERN LONDON

113

POLISH LONDON

From the eighteenth century onwards, Poland's history of partition, invasion and resistance, created a Polish presence in London – a self-contained, close-knit community, preoccupied with the military. But following the collapse of communism in Poland, business opportunities for British-born Poles have increased, and the former sense of exile has now began to fail.

In 1765, Poland was divided up between Austria, Prussia and Russia. Many Polish émigrés fled to France and a few to England, so starting a pattern of political exile. A succession of failed insurrections in 1830–1, 1848 and 1863–4 brought more exiles to Britain. In Highgate Cemetery, White Eagle Hill is the resting place of the leaders of the failed 1863–4 uprising; Joseph Conrad emigrated first to France and then to Britain after his father's arrest in the period prior to that rebellion. Some Poles came to Britain for purely economic reasons, taking on jobs as artisans or labourers. By the late nineteenth century, a Polish Christian community in London was centred around the Polish Catholic church on Devonia Road in Islington, Our Lady of Czestochowa. Large numbers of Polish Jews entered Britain during this period but they became assimilated into the Jewish community.

The real increase in Britain's Polish cummunity – swelling its numbers from 5,000 to tens of thousands – came with the Second World War. Following the German invasion in September 1939, over 30,000 Poles from the government and the military came to Britain. and a Polish Government-in-Exile under Prime Minister Sikorski was declared. Operational headquarters were set up around South Kensington and the Polish Air Force fought alongside the RAF. Their contribution was extensive: during the Battle of Britain one in seven of the German planes shot down was despatched by Polish airmen. A memorial to the 1,241 Polish airmen who died stands on the edge of Northolt Airport.

The Soviet occupation of Poland and the Treaty of Yalta dispossessed thousands of Poles by handing over Eastern Poland to the Soviet Union, so many Poles who had come to Britain to fight in the war stayed on. The British government offered free domicile to the 250,000 Poles (and their families) who had fought under British command, and over 150,000 accepted. Offers of British nationality were usually refused by Poles on patriotic grounds, in an effort to keep the political situation in Poland a 'live' issue. The Polish community looked back with both bitterness and nostalgia at what had once been theirs. The completion in 1982 of POSK, the Polish Social and Cultural Centre, at considerable expense, is a visible monument to its unity. The Catholic Church strengthened existing bonds; there are now around 12 Polish Catholic centres and churches in London.

High post-war property prices created a move west from Kensington to Earls Court, and Cromwell Road became known as the 'Polish Corridor'. Polish clubs founded during the war, such as the former magnificent White Eagle Club in Knightsbridge and the aristocratic Ognisko on Exhibition Road, had provided community focal points, but again rising costs edged the Polish community out into Balham, Chiswick and Ealing. Many of the upper and middle-class Poles (who constituted the majority of the community) had to adapt to difficult circumstances following the war. The second and third generations, while continuing to be linked to the Polish community, learnt English and as a result, became less dependent on it as their cultural focus shifted.

Korona Delicatessen

POLISH CUISINE

The popular perception of Polish cuisine as hearty winter food is a realistic one. The bitter Polish winters mean that many of the essential ingredients are those that can be stored or preserved: grains, root vegetables, sauerkraut, dried mushrooms, and salted and pickled herrings. Flavourful, warming stews and soups are popular, with soups such as krupnik (barley soup), yellow-pea soup and barley soup dating back to the Middle Ages.

Polish food is often described as Russian-influenced. This is a generalisation resented by the Poles, although the cuisines do share many dishes, ingredients and characteristic flavours. Other influences on Polish food, however, include Italian (traced back to the 1518 marriage of King Sigismund to Bona Sforza) and French, with one of the earliest cookbooks published in Poland, *The Perfect Cook*, being translated from the French.

Meat has always been highly valued in Polish cookery, a sad irony during the post-war years when meat was rationed and scarce. Every bit is used, producing the famous sausages, hams, black puddings, tongues and brawn. The Poles also enjoy game, traditionally hunted in their homeland's numerous forests. Bigos, or huntsman's stew, is a famous dish, made from game, sauerkraut and sausages. When Bona Sforza and her Italian retinue came to live in Poland, they were reputedly horrified at the amount of meat consumed by the Poles. The Italians introduced salads and certain vegetables, and even today 'wloscyzna', the word for basic green vegetables, means 'things Italian'.

Grains and cereals have always been important crops for the Poles, and rye bread is a staple. In her fascinating book *Old Polish Traditions in the Kitchen and at the Table*, Maria Lemnis writes, 'The popularity of bread in Poland is manifested in the numerous old sayings, e.g. 'bread unites the strongest'; 'bread cries when eaten for free'; 'bread obtained for labour is tasty and filling'; or, sharper in tone, 'whomever bread harms, a stick can cure'. Cereals such as millet, barley and buckwheat are used widely in dishes from soups to kasha, a purée of cooked grains.

The Catholic Church has had a marked influence on Polish cooking. Catholic festivals such as Christmas and Easter are celebrated with a host of special dishes and cakes. The austerity of the various fasts laid down by the church is also an influence, with fish and mushroom dishes eaten instead of meat at certain times of the year. Christmas Eve, for example, is traditionally celebrated with a feast including carp or pike.

Because of the grim economic situation and political isolation following the Second World War, Polish cookery remained frozen in time, restricted by severe food shortages and closed to foreign influences. The recent political changes and the opening up of trade means that Polish cuisine may again begin to change and develop.

GLOSSARY

Buckwheat: a triangular brown-green grain. Buckwheat flour is used in blinis.

Cakes: Cakes and pastries are an important feature of Polish life, and a huge variety is made, with some traditionally eaten at Christmas and Easter. Babka, a famous Easter yeast cake with a distinctive fluted shape; cheesecake, traditionally baked and not oversweet; makowiec, poppy-seed roll; mazurek: flat, traditionally rectangular cakes eaten at Easter; and paczki: Polish doughnuts, often filled with plum jam.

Caraway seeds: tiny, ridged brown seeds, with an aniseed flavour.

Curd cheese: a slightly tangy soft cheese made from curds, used in pierogi and cheesecake.

Dill: a caraway-flavoured herb with delicate, feathery fronds.

Dried mushrooms: hunting for wild mushrooms is a national pastime in Poland. Fresh wild mushrooms are rarely found in the shops, but both dried and pickled mushrooms are widely available.

Juniper berries: aromatic, blue-black berries, used with game.

Kohlrabi: a plump, rounded vegetable, either pale green or deep purple, called a 'cabbage-turnip' by Jane Grigson.

Pierogi: filled pasta pouches, often called Polish ravioli.

Pinhead barley: fine-grained barley.

Polish pure spirit: a powerful spirit – 168 proof – used to make vodka.

Poppy seeds: tiny white or purple-blue seeds, used in vast quantities in Polish baking.

Rye bread: a Polish fundamental. Rich-flavoured, dark brown Ukranian rye is distinctive.

Sauerkraut: pickled, shredded cabbage with a sharp flavour, available fresh or bottled.

Sausages: boiling ring, loops of spicy sausages; kabanos: long, thin pork sausages; kielbasa, pork and beef sausage flavoured with garlic; krakowska: garlic sausage, eaten as a salami.

Vodka: flavoured vodkas in Poland include: honey, lemon, sliwowica (prune), winiak (matured in wine barrels), wisniak (cherry), and zubrowska (bison-grass, easily identifiable because of the blades of long grass in the bottle).

Buckwheat

POLISH LONDON

FOODSHOPS

Polish food shops have been an important part of the self-contained Polish community in London. As one Polish lady said, 'We Poles like our food', and the shops provide essentials such as rye bread, sausages and cakes as well as acting as a local meeting place. Rumour has it that one Polish shop had a sign declaring 'English Spoken Here'. As the Polish community is declining in size, Polish food shops are becoming scarcer. Some have started to offer 'continental' foodstuffs in addition to Polish ingredients. Many of those listed below have been trading for years and have a pleasantly old-fashioned air about them.

NORTH

Austrian Sausage Centre
10A Belmont Street, NW1
(020-7-267 3601)
Tube: Chalk Farm
Open: Mon-Fri 7am-5pm; Sat 7am-1pm
Hidden away on an industrial estate, this functional retail outlet attracts East European ex-pat and English old age pensioners, drawn by the huge array of sausages and cooked and cured meats from brine to kielbasa.

SOUTH

Korona Delicatessen
30 Streatham High Road, SW16
(020-8-769 6647)
BR: Streatham Hill;
Bus: 159, 109 or 133
Open: Mon-Fri 9am-7pm;
Sat 9am-6pm; Sun 9am-1.30pm
Well-established for around 50 years now, this is a pleasantly old-fashioned shop with a fine range of Polish foodstuffs. It is especially noted for its cakes, which include baked cheesecake, chocolate-coated honey cake, poppyseed cakes and Easter specialities such as babka. Specialities include homemade pierogi, filled with curd cheese; meat, sauerkraut and wild mushrooms; stuffed cabbage and flavoured vodkas and gold wasser liqueur complete with flecks of real gold! Owners Mr and Mrs Wicinska are both knowledgeable and helpful.

Panadam Delicatessen
2 Marius Road, SW17
(020-8-673 4062)
Tube: Balham
Open: Tue & Thur-Sat 9.30am-5.45pm;
Wed 9.30am-1pm; Sun 10am-1.30pm
A charming 20 year-old delicatessen serving Balham's large Polish community. The deli-counter offers a good selection of Polish sausages, meats and herrings, and there is a range of rye breads and cakes. The Sunday opening is explained by the presence round the corner of the Polish church of Christ the King.

WEST

Adam and Agusia
258 King Street, W6
(020-8-741 8268)
Tube: Ravenscourt Park
Open: Mon-Fri 8am-10pm;
Sat 10am-10pm; Sun 11am-8pm
A shop-cum-café-cum-restaurant with a delicatessen counter selling Polish sausages, sweets, cakes, Krakus jams and pickles. Polish customers sit at the tables reading Polish newspapers and watching Polish satellite TV.

Enca Foods
2 Salisbury Pavement
Dawes Road, SW6
(020-7-385 5762)
Tube: Fulham Broadway
Open: Mon-Fri 7am-6pm; Sat 9am-6pm
Discreetly hidden behind what looks like
garage doors is a well-established, family-run
Polish food supplier. It is famous for the 30
types of sausages and cooked and cured
meats made on the premises – an appetising,
savoury smell permeates the shop. Meat is
delivered to the back door to be
transformed into specialities such as pork
brawn or roasted pork poledwica. There is
also a basic grocery stock of Central
European foodstuffs: ryebreads, cakes,
pickles and jams.

Parade Delicatessen
8 Central Buildings
The Broadway, W5
(020-8-567 9066)
Tube: Ealing Broadway
Open: Mon-Fri 9.15am-6pm;
Sat 9.15am-5pm

This attractive, roomy shop, directly
opposite Ealing Broadway station, caters for
the local Polish community as a continental
deli with a Polish slant. The delicatessen
counter contains Polish sausages and cured
meats, a variety of herrings, curd cheese and
pierogi. There is also rye bread, Polish cakes
and groceries such as Polish honey, packet
soups, seeds and pulses.

Prima Delicatessen
192 North End Road, W14
(020-7-385 2070)
Tube: West Kensington
Open: Mon-Thur & Sat 9.30am-6pm;
Fri 9.30am-7pm
Founded in 1948, this old-fashioned corner
shop is warmly recommended by Polish
friends. It has an excellent stock of Polish
ingredients: a large counter is filled with
sausages and smoked meats, rye breads,
cakes and pastries. The chilled section offers
pickled wild mushrooms and there is a rack
of pulses and seeds such as buckwheat and
poppy seeds.

POLISH LONDON

119

EATING PLACES

Many of London's best-known Polish eating places are housed in veteran clubs or institutions – a sign of how closely-knit the Polish community used to be.

CENTRAL

Daquise ££
20 Thurloe Street, SW7
(020-7-589 6117)
Tube: South Kensington
This sedate café has been a popular Polish meeting place since it was founded in the 1940s and is now an institution. The furniture and fittings, the Polish clientele and the elderly staff, complete the impression that nothing much has changed since the 1950s. The menu offers down-to-earth Polish food such as pierogi and apple strudel.

Ognisko Polskie £££
(Polish Hearth Club)
55 Princes Gate
Exhibition Road SW7
(020-7–589 4635)
Tube: South Kensington
Housed in an elegant high-ceilinged room, the restaurant at this famous Polish club is a bastion of excellent Polish food. The menu offers dishes including barszcz, bigos or pierogi, which can be washed down with flavoured vodkas.

NORTH

Primrose Brasserie ££
101 Regent's Park Road, NW1
(020-7–483 3765)
Tube: Chalk Farm
A large, relaxed, friendly restaurant which offers huge portions of tasty Polish food at very reasonable prices.

Zamoyski ££
86 Fleet Road, NW3
(020-7-794 4792)
Tube: Belsize Park
A pleasant and intimate wine bar and restaurant offering traditional Polish food and vodkas.

WEST

Adam & Agusia £
258 King Street, W6
(020-8-741 8268)
Tube: Ravenscourt Park
A small, unpretentious café, just a few doors down from the Polish Cultural Centre, offering good down-to-earth fare.

Café Grove £
65 The Grove, W5
(020-8-840 3276)
Tube: Ealing Broadway
A pretty café serving the local Polish community and offering a tempting range of Polish cakes and savoury dishes.

Lowiczanka (POSK) £
238-46 King Street, W6
(020-8-741 3225)
Tube: Ravenscourt Park
Inside the Polish Social and Cultural Centre is this large restaurant, with a typically Polish menu. Service can be slow so be prepared for a leisurely meal. Prices are reasonable, especially the set lunch.

Wodka £££
12 St Albans Grove, W8
(020-7-937 6513)
Tube: Kensington High Street
A sleek New-Wave Polish restaurant serving distinctly upmarket food at corresponding prices. As the name implies, they also serve a range of flavoured vodkas.

COOKBOOKS

**The Food and Cooking
of Eastern Europe**
Lesley Chamberlain
A clearly-written, overall look at East-
European cookery.

The Polish Kitchen
Mary Pininska
A well-written, knowledgeable book on
Polish cookery, with appetising recipes.

POLISH LONDON

121

SOUTH-EAST ASIAN LONDON

T he South-East Asian community in London is widespread and diverse, reflecting the variety of its national origins. The term 'South-East Asia' encompassess Indonesia, Malaysia, the Philippines, Singapore, Thailand and Vietnam. There is no obvious centre, an equivalent to Gerrard Street for the Chinese, but Peckham is a focal point for the Vietnamese, and Earls Court a centre for the Filipino community.

Lack of economic opportunities in their own countries is the main reason for many South-East Asians seeking work in Britain, demonstrated most tragically by the Vietnamese boat people. Much of their work is found in the catering or hotel industries, but the last two Immigration Acts have made it much harder for people from these countries to enter Britain.

SOUTH-EAST ASIAN CUISINE

The term, 'South-East Asian cuisine' is the blanket term used to describe the cuisines of Indonesia, Malaysia, the Philippines, Singapore, Thailand and Vietnam – a simple way to describe a complex set of overlapping national cuisines. Seemingly no dish has a single recipe in South-East Asia: variations abound from country to country, region to region and family to family. Satay in Thailand may be served with toast and a chilli-based dipping sauce, whereas the Indonesian version comes with a spicy peanut sauce, cucumber and cubes of compressed rice. Differences stem from race and religion with, for example pork avoided by the Muslim Malays but enjoyed by the Chinese. These variations help create a rich and diverse set of cuisines, but there are certain shared characteristics.

Both Chinese and Indian cuisines have influenced South-East Asian food in cooking techniques and ingredients. From China comes the balancing of five flavours: sweet, sour, hot, salty and bitter; and, from India, the use of spices and curry pastes. Like both Chinese and Indian cuisines, South-East Asian cuisine is mainly rice-based.

Certain ingredients provide unique flavours that distinguish South-East Asian cooking. Coconut milk, extracted from the flesh of the versatile coconut, is a key ingredient. It is widely used in both savoury and sweet dishes as a marinade, a stock, a curry-base and a dairy equivalent. Fragrant aromatics have a citrus quality: lemon grass, lime juice, kaffir lime leaves and rind. To the Asian trinity of onion, garlic and ginger are added the more subtle rhizomes, galingal and krachai. Chillies, introduced by the Portuguese and Spanish in the sixteenth century, provide a characteristic South-East Asian 'hot' kick.

Seafood is important in South-East Asian cooking and found in abundance. In its dried and fermented forms seafood is used to add saltiness to food. Fish sauce often replaces soy sauce in Thailand, the Philippines and Vietnam, while pungent shrimp paste is used throughout South-East Asia.

Indonesian and Malay cooking are often grouped together, as the majority religion in both countries is Islam. Singapore is distinguished culinarily by Nonya or Straits Chinese cuisine, a unique blend of heavily-spiced dishes combining Chinese and Malay ingredients and techniques. Thai cooking, with its emphasis on aesthetic presentation, is marked by its use of aromatic herbs such as coriander roots, Thai mint and several varieties of basil. Filipino cuisine stands out from the rest of South-East Asia, as it was influenced by the Spanish colonisation of the country from 1521 to 1898, and subsequent American occupation until 1946. The Spanish influence is apparent in Filipino dishes such as adobo and paella while American influences crop up in a predeliction for condensed milk and apple pie. Brightly-coloured rice cakes and desserts are also popular, made with ingredients such as makapuno, soft-fleshed coconut. Vietnamese cuisine is seen to stem largely from the Chinese, with basic ingredients for Vietnamese cooking available in Chinese supermarkets. Vietnamese fish sauce (nuoc mam) is a key ingredient and the generous use of fresh herbs, such as dill and mint, is another distinguishing feature.

SOUTH-EAST ASIAN LONDON

GLOSSARY

Agar agar: a vegetarian setting agent obtained from seaweed which does not require refrigeration to set, available in either powdered form or translucent strands. Filipino agar agar (gulaman) comes in bright pink and yellow to add colour to desserts.

Annatto (achuete): small red seeds which impart an orange colour.

Banana leaves: used to wrap foods in a similiar way to kitchen foil, but also adding flavour to whatever is cooked within.

Basil: a herb used in Indonesian, Thai and Vietnamese cuisines. In Thailand one finds bai horapa (similar to European sweet basil), bai mangluk, and bai garapo or holy basil.

Bean curd (tahu, tokua): a nutritious soya-bean product. Fresh, ivory-coloured bean curd has a firm, custard texture and bland flavour and is sold packed in water. Deep-fried bean curd has a golden colour and spongy texture. Both are found in the chilled section.

Candlenuts (kemiri, buah keras): large, white, waxy nuts, used to thicken curry pastes, sold unshelled. Raw macadamia nuts are the closest substitute.

Chilli paste (nam prik pow): a thick sauce made from chillies, onions and sugar.

Chillies (prik, cabe, sili labuyo): introduced from South America by the Portuguese and Spanish in the sixteenth century, chillies are an essential ingredient in South-East Asian cookery. Generally the smallest are the hottest, for instance, the tiny Thai bird's eye chillies.

Coconut milk (santen): this thick white 'milk' is made from the grated flesh of the coconut and not from the cloudy water found inside the coconut. In South-East Asia freshly-made coconut milk is sold in markets; here, tinned coconut milk is the best option widely available. Creamed coconut and coconut milk powder, both of which need mixing with hot water, are the other options.

Coriander (cilantro, Chinese parsley, daun ketumbar, pak chee): this green flat-leafed herb, similar in appearance to continental parsley, has a distinctive sharp flavour. Both the seeds and the leaves are used throughout South-East Asia.

Custard apple (sweet-sop): an apple-shaped, green-skinned fruit with creamy flesh and plentiful small seeds.

Durian: a notorious large, spiky, green-skinned fruit, prized as a delicacy throughout South-East Asia. It is notable for its pungent smell, described as a cross between Camembert and turpentine and, as a result, is banned on airlines.

Fish sauce (nam pla, nuoc mam, patis): a thin, brown salty liquid, produced from compressed shrimps or small fish, and used similarly to soy sauce as a salty flavouring.

Galingal (Siamese ginger, kenguas, languas, ka): a fleshy rhizome, resembling a creamy-coloured root ginger with pink nodules, and a sharp, medicinal aroma. Available fresh or dried, either in pieces or in powder form (Laos powder).

Ginger: a brown-skinned rhizome, noted for its aromatic flavour and digestive qualities. Lesser ginger (krachai in Thai) is a milder relation and, while similarly-coloured, comes in clusters of small 'fingers'.

Lemongrass

Jackfruit: bulky, football-sized fruit with a thick green skin covered in prickles, similar in appearance to durian. Yellow jackfruit flesh is available tinned.

Kaffir limes (jeruk purut, makrut): large limes with a bumpy, dark-green skin. The glossy lime leaves, sold in bunches or packets of loose leaves, are used in South-East Asian cooking and add a distinctive citrus flavour.

Kalamansi: small, round, green citrus fruits used in the Philippines to make a refreshing drink.

Kangkong: water-convolvulus leaves, eaten as a green vegetable.

Lemon grass (serai, sereh, takrai): a fibrous grey-green grass with a white bulbous base and subtle citrus flavour.

Macapuno: a type of coconut with soft, slightly sticky flesh, used in Filipino desserts.

Mango: an orange-fleshed, fragrant fruit, eaten fresh and used in desserts. Pale orange Thai mangoes are particularly prized for their delicate flavour and scoopable flesh.

Mangosteen: an apple-sized fruit with thick purple skin which, despite its name, is no relation to the mango. Inside, it contains white pulpy segments with a delicate, perfumed flavour.

Milkfish (bangus): a bony, white-fleshed fish, cultivated and eaten extensively in the Philippines.

Mooli (daikon): a large, long white radish with crisp flesh.

Noodles: cellophane noodles (also known as beanthread, glass or transparent noodles) are fine threadlike noodles made from mung beans, which need soaking before they can be easily cut; yellow egg noodles (available fresh and dried); dried white rice noodles and vermicelli; river rice or sarhor noodles, made from ground rice and water. Fresh river rice noodles are sold in clear packets, usually stored near the chilled section.

Palm sugar (gula melaka): a caramel-flavoured, dark brown sugar made from the coconut palm flower, sold in small, hard cylinderical blocks.

Pandan leaves: long, thin, dark-green screwpine leaves, sold fresh in bunches. They add a unique, slightly nutty flavour and green colouring to desserts.

Pawpaw (papaya): a gourd-like fruit, which comes in varying sizes and colours from deep green to orange. Green pawpaw is used in salads by the Thais.

Pea aubergine: tiny pea-sized aubergines with a sharp, bitter taste, used especially in Thai cooking.

Pomelo (shaddock): the largest of the citrus fruits, resembling a huge grapefruit with a flattened end; used in Thai salads.

Prawn crackers (krupuk): flat wafers which puff up when fried. Emping are a slightly bitter Indonesian version, made with melinjo nuts, and used to garnish gado gado salad.

Rambutan: a fruit resembling a hairy, red egg – the name comes from 'rambut', Malay for 'hair'. Inside is a translucent, juicy egg-shaped fruit, prized for its refreshing qualities.

Rice: long-grain rice is commonly used, with the best coming from Thailand. The phrase 'perfumed rice' is an indicator of quality. Short-grained white and black glutinous rice is also used in both savoury and sweet dishes.

Shrimps, dried: small, shelled, dried pink shrimps, with a strong salty flavour.

Shrimp paste (blachan, terasi, bagoong, kapee, mam tan): a paste made from fermented shrimps, available in many forms, from solid, brown blocks to bottled pink-grey liquid. It has an extremely pungent smell and should be stored in an airtight container.

Soy sauce: a dark brown, salty liquid made from fermented soya beans, available as thin, salty Light Soy Sauce or as thicker, sweeter Dark Soy Sauce. Kecap manis is a thick, sweet Indonesian soy sauce.

Starfruit (carambola): a ridged, fleshy fruit which when sliced produces star-shaped slices.

Straw mushrooms: cone-shaped mushrooms, usually available canned.

Tamarind (asam, mak kum): a bean-like fruit from the tamarind tree, available in lumps of de-seeded pulp, and used to add tartness to dishes. Tamarind sauce, although slightly salty, is a convenient version. 'Tamarind slices', from a different fruit with similar qualities, is also available.

Tempe: a pressed fermented soya bean product, with a nutty taste.

Turmeric: a slender, brown-skinned rhizome, with a deep orange flesh. Widely available in dried powdered form, or occasionally found fresh.

Ube: a bright purple, sweet yam used in Filipino cookery.

Yard-long beans: as the name implies, these are long green beans, commonly cut into short lengths before cooking.

FOODSHOPS

Traditionally the more plentiful Chinese supermakets have acted as umbrella suppliers, carrying basic South-East Asian ingredients. With the recent boom in Thai cookery, major supermarket chains are also starting to stock ingredients such as tinned coconut milk and fresh lemon grass. For the more unusual items, especially vegetables and herbs, it is necessary to track down a specialist South-East Asian shop.

CENTRAL

See Woo
19 Lisle Street, WC2
(020-7-439 8325)
Tube: Leicester Square
Open: Mon-Sun 10am-8pm
Of all Soho's Chinese supermarkets, See Woo is the most consistently recommended for its range of South-East Asian foodstuffs. The greengrocer's section regularly stocks items such as fresh turmeric, kaffir limes and lime leaves and galingal.

EAST

Alan's Chinese & Vietnamese Grocery
199 East India Dock Road, E14
(020-7-515 8909)
DLR: All Saints
Open: Daily 10am-10pm
A small Vietnamese grocery with an excellent range of Vietnamese foodstuffs, from bunches of fresh dill, mint and coriander to a huge range of dried noodles.

NORTH-WEST

Hopewell Emporium
2f Dyne Road, NW6
(020-7-624 5473)
Tube: Kilburn
Open: Mon & Wed-Sun 7am-10.30pm
This large South-East Asian foodstore, run with relaxed friendliness by Tony, specialises in Indonesian ingredients such as tempeh and emping, and caters to the North London Indonesian community whose embassy staff live mainly in Hendon. Fresh produce include snake beans, banana leaves and pea aubergines, while there is also an excellent range of bottled, tinned and packeted ingredients.

Maysun Market
869 Finchley Road
(020 8 455 4773)
Tube: Golders Green
Open: Mon-Sat 9am-7.30pm
This small shop stocks a selection of South-East Asian ingredients (predominantly tinned, bottled, frozen or dried) which range from frozen seafood and packets of pig's blood to tins of Alphonso mango pulp.

Wing Yip (London) Ltd
395 Edgware Road, NW2
(020-8-450 0422)
Tube: Colindale
Open: Mon-Sat 9.30am-7pm;
Sun 11.30am-5.30pm
This enormous supermarket at Staples Corner contains an impressive range of South-East Asian ingredients, and is particularly strong on bottled, tinned, dried and frozen foods. The greengrocer's section, although small, stocks more unusual items including pandan leaves, Thai basil and fresh tamarind.

SOUTH-EAST

Wing Thai Supermarket
13 Electric Avenue, SW9
(020-7-738 5898)
Tube: Brixton
Open: Mon-Sat 10am-7pm

SOUTH-EAST ASIAN LONDON

Tucked away behind the bustling fruit and veg stalls outside, this roomy store has a small fresh produce section, but is very strong on bottled, tinned and frozen goods with a range of Vietnamese products such as dried rice wrappers.

SOUTH-WEST LONDON

Talad Thai
320 Upper Richmond Road, SW15
(020-8-789 8084)
BR: Putney
Open: Mon-Sat 9am-10.30pm;
Sun 10am-8pm
Upstairs functions as a Thai take-away while downstairs is a basement supermarket with a small back room of fresh vegetables, herbs and fruits – such as Thai basils and pea aubergines. The large freezer section contains meat and seafood while the shelves are lined with noodles, condiments, tinned vegetables and coconut milk. The manageress is friendly and helpful and there are Thai cookery demonstations every Sunday morning.

Wang Thai Market
101-103 Kew Road, TW9
(020-8-332 2959/8)
Tube: Richmond
Open: Mon-Sat 10am-8pm; Sun 11am-6pm
Now in its tenth year, this large, roomy store has every thing you could want for Thai cooking, from fresh pea aubergines and fragrant Thai basil to bottles of fish sauce and tins of coconut milk. The counter has large woven baskets displaying dwarf bananas, Thai pumpkins and sweet tamarind pods. Staff are very friendly and helpful and there are also picture charts identifying ingredients. For those in a hurry, the large freezer contains authentically tasty, ready-made Thai meals, such as chicken in pandan leaves and green chicken curry.

WEST

Manila Supermarket
11-12 Hogarth Place
(020-7-373 8305)
Tube: Earls Court
Open: Mon-Sun 9am-9pm
As the name and the stacks of *The Filipino* newspaper near the door suggest, this roomy store specialises in Filipino foodstuffs such as purple yam jam, coconut spread and pork sausages, but also stocks an excellent range of general South-East Asian ingredients. One room contains freezers of grated cassava, fresh coconut milk, sweet potato leaves and a variety of fish and seafood. Greengrocer's items include chillies, galingal and banana leaves. Staff are friendly.

Sri Thai
56 Shepherd's Bush Road, W6
(020-7-602 0621)
Tube: Shepherds Bush
Open: Mon-Sun 9am-7pm
This clearly-arranged shop h.. a great selection of Thai ingredients and is run with friendly courtesy by Mr and Mrs Threpprasits. Tuesday is the best day to visit for fresh vegetables and herbs jet .. in from Thailand, such as bitter melon and galingal.

Tawana
16-20 Chepstow Road, W2
(020-7-221 6316)
Tube: Bayswater
Open: Mon-Sun 9.30am-8pm
"There were only two Thai restaurants in London when we started 15 years ago," muses owner Mr Farooqi. Today, Thai food is very popular and his roomy, well-stocked shop does a roaring business in Thai staples such as kaffir lime leaves, coconut milk and lemon grass. Wednesdays and Saturdays are the best days for fresh produce flown in from Thailand, including pea aubergines, banana leaves and holy basil.
Also at: *243-245 Plaistow Road, E15*

Sri Thai

EATING PLACES

W ith Pacific Rim fusion-cooking all the rage, authentic South-East Asian food in London is pretty scarce. With delicious ingredients such as lemongrass, lime leaves and coconut milk to use, it's not so much that the majority of food on offer is unpleasant – rather that it lacks the range of flavours and gutsiness of the genuine article.

CENTRAL

Melati *££*
21 Great Windmill Street, W1
(020-7-437 2745)
Tube: Piccadilly Circus
Tucked away among the strip joints, this veteran Indonesian and Malay restaurant continues to be popular and busy. Indonesian dishes, such as beef rendang, are particularly good.

Satay House *££*
13 Sale Place, W2
(020-7-723 6763)
Tube: Edgware Road or Paddington
Tucked away in a quiet side street, this is a peaceful place in which to enjoy Malaysian dishes such as murtabak (mince-stuffed flat bread) and tasty char kway teow. Sweet tooths can be satisfied with authentic versions of pulot hitam or ice kacang.

Selasih *££*
114 Seymour Place, W1
(020-7-224 8816)
Tube: Edgware Road
A bargain lunchtime buffet means that this small, friendly, pretty restaurant fills up fast with local office workers. It's well worth ordering à la carte, however, to sample excellent versions of classic dishes such as nasi lemak.

Silks and Spice *££*
23 Foley Street, W1
(020-7-636 2718)
Tube: Goodge Street,
Great Portland Street or Oxford Street
An attractively-styled restaurant with an extensive menu of South-East Asian dishes, ranging from Malay to Thai. Set-price lunches are good value and the food is flavourful and prettily presented.
Also at:
103 Boundary Road, NW8
28 Chalk Farm Road, NW1
95 Chiswick High Road, W4

Singapore Garden *£££*
154-156 Gloucester Place, NW1
(020-7-723 8233)
Tube: Baker Street
This smart basement restaurant – a branch of the Swiss Cottage restaurant – offers Singaporean dishes such as laksa and char kway teow. The Regent's Park Hotel upstairs is aimed at Singaporean business people who then move downstairs to dine on tasty home-style food.

EAST

Thai Garden *££*
249 Globe Road, E2
(020-8-981 5748)
Tube: Bethnal Green
A small, friendly Thai restaurant serving up flavourful seafood and vegetarian dishes, using authentic ingredients.

SOUTH-EAST ASIAN LONDON

NORTH

O's Thai Cafe   £.£.
10 Topsfield Parade, N8
(020-8-348 6898)
Tube: Finsbury Park, then the W7 bus
Bright, light and funky, O's attracts a stream
of Crouch End diners drawn by the chance
to try tasty Thai dishes (such as green
chicken curry) at very reasonable prices.

NORTH-WEST

Singapore Garden   £.£.£.
83-83a Fairfax Road, NW6
(020-7-328 5314)
Tube: Swiss Cottage
A loyal multi-cultural clientele testifies to
this smart restaurant's commitment to
admirably authentic Singaporean food. The
menu offers predominantly Chinese food,
but includes a range of South-East Asian
delicacies such as mouth-watering and
gloriously messy chilli crab, excellent satay
and oyster omelette, and the best cendol (a
coconut milk drink) in town.

WEST

Bedlington Cafe   £.£.
24 Fauconberg Road, W4
(020-8-994 1965)
Tube: Chiswick Park or Turnham Green, then
the E3 or E4 bus
Originally a standard café in the day offering
Thai food at night, it now does tasty Thai
food at both lunch and dinnertime. Prices
are low and it remains unlicensed, but as its
fame has spread far beyond Chiswick,
booking is now essential.

Makan   £.
270 Portobello Road, W10
(020-8-960 5169)
Tube: Ladbroke Grove
Situated under the Westway flyover, this
relaxed and friendly Malaysian eaterie offers
cheap, tasty dishes from freshly-made roti
canai to spicy fried chicken.

COOKBOOKS

Far Eastern Cookery
Madhur Jaffrey
A well-written exploration of Asian cookery
with clear, useable recipes.

Indonesian Food and Cookery
Sri Own
An authoritative and in-depth book.

Thai Cooking
Jennifer Brennan
A classic book on Thai cuisine, lovingly and
knowledgeably written.

SOUTH-EAST ASIAN LONDON

SPANISH & PORTUGUESE LONDON

Although a Spanish presence in London can be traced back to the Middle Ages, the real growth in the capital's Spanish and Portuguese communities came in the twentieth century. Following the Spanish Civil War (1936–9), many Spanish refugees and political exiles came to Britain. Republican exiles set up El Hogar Espanol (The Spanish House) in Bayswater: a cultural, social and political focal point. In addition to political reasons for coming to Britain, economic ones also played their part. During the 1950s and 1960s, millions of working-class Spaniards were forced to leave Spain and look for work abroad because of the lack of opportunities at home. The area around Ladbroke Grove was a focal point for the Spanish community. Many of the Spanish in Britain are from Galicia, the north-west coastal region of Spain which has a seafaring and travelling tradition and which suffered in the post-war depression. The area around Ladbroke Grove was a focal point for the Spanish community.

Despite the fact that Portugal is Britain's oldest ally (a tie dating back to the Treaty of Windsor in 1386) the Portuguese community in London is small. It was created primarily after the Second World War as a result of a lack of economic opportunities in Portugal.

The main Iberian community is in West London, with Golborne Road and Portobello being the two main thoroughfares. On these roads, the community is served by a Spanish school and Spanish and Portuguese delicatessens, and cafés and bars in which to meet other members of the community.

SPANISH & PORTUGUESE CUISINE

Both Spanish and Portuguese cookery share many characteristic ingredients: salted cod, paprika sausages, rice, beans, garlic and olive oil. The Moorish occupation of the Iberian Peninsula from AD 711 has left its mark on the sweets of both countries, with ground almonds and egg yolks used in desserts and cakes such as the Portuguese touchino de ceu or Spanish tarta de naranja.

Seafood is important in both cuisines, with an extensive range fished on the countries' long coastlines. Many of the famous regional dishes are seafood-based, such as zarzuela (Catalan seafood stew), marmitako (Basque bonito soup) and Northern-Portuguese caldeirada. There is no squeamishness when it comes to seafood. Lampreys are eaten in Northern Portugal in a famous dish, lapreia a moda do Minho; while Spanish calamares en su tinta, calls for squid to be cooked in its own black ink. Absolute freshness is demanded and one traditional Spanish fish dish is nicknamed mato mulo (mule killer) because the fish used in it had to be rushed by mule from the coast to Madrid.

There are some obvious differences between the cuisines and national dishes. From Portugal's former colonies comes spices and flavourings such as spicy piri piri sauce – used in both Brazil and East Africa. Tapas, however, are quintessentially Spanish. The term means 'little lid' and is thought to come from the bar tradition of covering glasses with a saucer of olives or nuts. Bars vie with each other to offer good tapas and the discerning Spanish, who both enjoy their food and take it seriously, hunt out their favourites with a passion.

Both Spain and Portugal retain a strong sense of regionalism, with traditional dishes still cherished. Many recipes feature a place name, such as de salmao a Lisboeta, or fabada Asturiana. As in Italian cuisine, certain areas or towns are known for the quality of their food, with the best Spanish seafood from Cadiz or Galicia and the best Portuguese caldo verde from the Minho.

GLOSSARY

Aguardiente (orujo): a potent Spanish spirit, distilled from the left-over grapes and pips after wine has been made.

Anchovies (boquerones, biqueiros): tiny cured fish, usually filleted, with a strong, salty flavour.

Capers (alcaparras): the unopened buds of a Mediterranean shrub, sold and used in their pickled form. Spain is the world's largest producer of capers.

Cava: sparkling Spanish wine made using the champagne method, with Cordoniu and Frexenet among the best producers.

Charcuterie: butifarra: a white Spanish sausage, spiced with cinnamon, cloves and nutmeg; chorizo or chourico: a range of paprika sausages, used in cooked dishes, to which they add a distinctive colour and flavour, or eaten as a salami; jamon de Serrano: a highly prized, salt-cured Spanish ham, the best of which is made from the acorn-fed pigs of the Estremadura region; lomo, cured pork loin from Spain; presunto: a fine salt-cured ham from Portugal, traditionally made from acorn-fed pigs from Tras-os-Montes.

Cheese: azeitaio, small Portuguese sheep's milk cream cheeses; cabrales: a famous Spanish blue-veined cheese, made from cow's milk and sometimes with sheep's or goat's milk added; evora: a creamy, strong, salty sheep's milk cheese from Portugal;

SPANISH & PORTUGUESE LONDON

idiazabal: a much-prized, semi-soft cheese with a dark rind made from sheep's milk in the Basque region of Spain; ilha, a Portuguese Cheddar-like cheese made from cow's milk; mahon, a flavourful Spanish semi-soft cow's milk cheese; manchego: one of Spain's best-known cheeses, made with sheep's milk and sold in three grades depending on age; roncal: a hard, Spanish, sheep's milk cheese; serra: a soft, Portuguese, sheep's milk cheese.

Chickpeas (garbanzos, grado): hazelnut-shaped, yellow peas.

Coriander (coentros): a sharp-flavoured green herb, similar in appearance to continental parsley, widely used in Portuguese cookery.

Madeira: a famous Portuguese fortified wine, from the island of Madeira.

Madelenas: small, sweet, golden-brown cakes, eaten for breakfast in Spain.

Olive oil: olive oil is produced in both Spain and Portugal and is the main cooking oil in both countries. Carbonell, with its elegant Art Nouveau labels, is one of Spain's famous brands.

Olives: green olives stuffed with anchovies are particularly popular in Spain.

Paprika: a bright red powder, made from ground sweet or spicy peppers and used as a spice.

Pine kernels (pinon, pinhao): small, ivory-coloured stone pine kernels, used in both sweet and savoury dishes.

Piri piri: a hot Portuguese sauce made from chillies, a culinary legacy from Portugal's colonial past.

Port: a fortified wine from the Douro valley in North-West Portugal. Its creation can be traced back to the early seventeenth century when, due to Anglo-French hostilities, Portuguese wine rather than French claret was exported to England.

Quince paste (membrillo, marmelo): a thick, golden, jelly-like paste made from quinces, eaten as a sweetmeat or as a classic accompaniment to cheese.

Rice: introduced by the Moors to Spain and Portugal in AD 711. Short-grain rice is used for Spanish paella.

Saffron: a costly spice made from the stigmas of a type of crocus, sold in either thread or powdered form.

Salt cod (bacalao, bacalhau): dried, salted cod traditionally eaten on Fridays for religious reasons. In Portugal it is regarded as a national delicacy and there is said to be a different bacalhau recipe for every day of the year. It should be soaked for 24–36 hours before cooking to remove excess salt.

Sherry: a classic Spanish wine named after the town of Jerez and imported by the British since the fifteenth century.

Tiger nut (chufa): a small, wrinkled rhizome from which horchata, a refreshing almond-flavoured drink thought to have been introduced by the Moors, is made.

Turron: Spanish nougat, available in two forms: alicante, crisp and textured with chopped nuts, or jijona, soft and crumbly, made from ground nuts. Traditionally this is a Christmas treat but it is now available all the year round.

Vinho verde: delicate effervescent wines, both white and red, which form around a quarter of Portugal's wine production.

Garcia R.& Sons

FOODSHOPS

As with the Italian food stores, many of these shops began as corner shops rather than delicatessens, selling everyday ingredients to their community.

CENTRAL

Delices de Portugal
43 Warwick Way, SW1
(020-7-630 5597)
Tube: Pimlico or Victoria
Open: Mon-Sat 8am-8pm; Sun 9am-2pm
This pretty delicatessen caters to hungry office workers, offering pasteis de bacalhau and a selection of Portuguese cakes and pastries as well as sandwiches. There is a large range of deli goods, including huge slabs of bacalhau (cut on demand), packets of 'flan' and a range of goat's cheeses.

Products from Spain
89 Charlotte Street, W1
(020-7-580 2905)
Tube: Goodge Street
Open: Mon-Fri 10am-5.30pm;
Sat 10am-1pm
This delightful Spanish delicatessen is a family business, acting as a showcase for the Lopez brothers' Spanish food import–export business, set up by their father over 30 years ago. The range of stock is both extensive and carefully selected: excellent jamon de Serrano, a range of chorizo sausgaes, pure saffron, Miau seafood products, Carbonell olive oil, cavas and turron. There are even paellera, in which to cook your paella. Service is courteous and helpful.

NORTH

Ferreira
40 Delancey Street, NW1
(020-7-485 2351)
Tube: Camden Town
Open: Mon-Sun 8am-10pm
A friendly Portuguese corner store which has something for everybody. On the counter is a selection of cakes such as pasteis de nata, inside are Portuguese cheeses and sausages, while behind are shelves of Portuguese breakfast cereals. In addition, there is a selection of tinned and bottled groceries, wines and slabs of bacalhau.

Villa Franca
3 Plender Street, NW1
(020-7-387 8236)
Tube: Camden Town
Open: Mon-Sat 8am-8.30pm;
Sun 8am-7pm
A small down-to-earth shop-cum-café selling a mixture of Portuguese and English patisserie plus a range of foodstuffs: bacalhau (stored beneath the counter), cured meats, soft drinks and cheeses such as queijo Evora. Downstairs is a smoking room from which blares the sound of Portuguese satellite TV.

Rias Altas
97 Frampton Street, NW8
(020-7-262 4340)
Tube: Edgware Road
Open: Mon-Sat 9.30am-8pm;
Sun 11.30am-2pm
A long, narrow Spanish delicatessen, well-stocked with foodstuffs such as Spanish cheeses, cured meats, bacalao and Spanish wines.

SPANISH & PORTUGUESE LONDON ·

SOUTH

Brindisa
3 Riverside Workshops
28 Park Street, SE1
(020-7-403 0282)
Tube: London Bridge
Open: the third Sat of each month 10am-5pm
Tucked away in a warehouse complex near
Borough Market, this Spanish wholesaler
has a stall at the market on the third
Saturday of every month. It offers an
interesting selection of very classy Spanish
foodstuffs, from pata negra salchichon and
delicious white tuna in olive oil to superior
almonds and turrons.

Sintra Delicatessen
146-48 Stockwell Road, SW9
(020-7-733 9402)
Tube: Stockwell
Open Mon-Sun 9am-8pm
The scent of bacalhau and the hum of
conversation evoke Portugal as you enter
this homely shop, which is attached to a
down-to-earth café and restaurant. There is
a good selection of foodstuffs: chourico,
presunto and morcela and Portuguese cakes
and bread. The shelves are lined with
Portuguese groceries: cereal, olive oil,
Portuguese wines and boxes of Ancora
crochet yarn.

WEST

Garcia R. & Sons
248 Portobello Road, W11
(020-7-221 6119)
Tube: Notting Hill or Ladbroke Road
Open: Tues-Sat 8.30am-6pm
The Garcia family have had a Spanish food-
shop on Portobello Road for over 40 years.
Their present shop is London's largest
Spanish delicatessen and retains a pleasantly
old-fashioned feel. The deli counter does a
roaring trade in Jamon Serrano and costly
Jamon Iberico (from acorn-fed black-footed

pigs), which are deftly sliced to order. In
addition, there are groceries such as chorizo
sausages, three different pimenton, paella
rice, tinned seafood, bacalao and olive oil.
Turrons are kept throughout the year, with
the range expanding at Christmas time.

Lisboa Delicatessen
54 Golborne Road, W10
(020-8-969 1052)
Tube: Westbourne Park
Open: Mon-Sat 9.30am-7.30pm;
Sun 10am-1pm
When Carlos Gomes opened this shop
around 20 years ago, it was the first
Portuguese delicatessen in London. All the
essential ingredients for Portuguese cooking
can be found in this characterful shop:
pungent bacalhau, pulses including Brazilian
black beans, sausages and trayfuls of pickled
and salted pig's trotters, snouts, tails and
ears. A back-room contains a selection of
Portuguese wines and spirits, including port.
The shelf space not devoted to foodstuffs is
piled with boxes of crochet thread 'to keep
the wives busy'!

Lisboa Patisserie
57 Golborne Road, W10
(020-8-968 5242)
Tube: Westbourne Park
Open: Mon-Sun 8am-8pm
Across the road from the delicatessen, this
small, popular patisserie supplies a constant
stream of customers with delicious
Portuguese pastries such as pasteis de nata
(custard tarts) and bolo arroz (rice cakes).

P. de la Fuente
288 Portobello Road, W10
(020-8-960 5687)
Tube: Notting Hill or Ladbroke Road
Open: Mon-Sat 9am-6pm
Just down the road from the large Spanish
College, is this small, down-to-earth
Spanish foodshop with a good stock of
essentials.

SPANISH & PORTUGUESE LONDON

137

COOKBOOKS

Portuguese Cookery
Ursula Bourne
A basic introduction to Portuguese cuisine.

The Spanish Kitchen
Nicholas Butcher
A knowledgeable book conveying the
regional diversity of Spanish cooking.

The Foods and Wines of Spain
Penelope Casas
An excellent, comprehensive and appetising
survey of Spanish cuisine.

**The Gastronomy of Spain
and Portugal**
Maite Manjon
A useful encyclopedia of Iberian food

The Food of Spain and Portugal
Elizabeth Lambert Ortiz
A knowledgeable look at Iberian cooking,
with accessible recipes.

Saltcod

EATING PLACES

CENTRAL

Moro £££££
34-36 Exmouth Market, EC1
(020-7-833 8336)
Tube: Farringdon
Much critical acclaim has greeted this stylish
restaurant, which draws on both Spanish and
North African cuisines to offer an inventive
menu. Delights include melt-in-the-mouth
crab brik and delicious sherry ice-cream.

NORTH

La Bota ££
31 Broadway Parade,
Tottenham Lane, N8
(020-8-340 3082)
Tube: Finsbury Park, then the W7 bus
A straightforward tapas bar which attracts a
lively crowd.

El Parador ££
245 Eversholt Street, NW1
(020-7-387 3789)
Tube: Camden Town
This tapas bar comes into its own in the
summer, when you can sit in the garden at
the back and sample a range of tapas washed
down with Spanish wines and beers.

SOUTH

The Gallery ££
256A Brixton Hill, SW2
(020-8-671 8311)
Tube: Brixton
Stockwell's Portuguese community are well
served by this friendly, down-to-earth
restaurant offering large portions of tasty,
authentic food.

Meson Don Felipe ££
53 The Cut, SE1
(020-7-928 3237)
Tube: Waterloo
A large, attractive tapas bar, with a central
counter piled high with appetising morsels.

Rebatos ££
169 South Lambeth Road, SW8
(020-7-735 6388)
Tube: Stockwell
An atmospheric and popular tapas bar, with
above-average tapas served at the front bar
and a large restaurant area at the back.

WEST

Galicia ££
323 Portobello Road, SW10
(020-8-969 3539)
Tube: Notting Hill or Ladbroke Grove
This atmospheric tapas bar-cum-restaurant,
popular with the local Spanish community,
specialises in food from Galicia, hence the
large number of fish and seafood dishes.

Lisboa Patisserie £
57 Golborne Road, W10
(020-8-968 5242)
Tube: Notting Hill or Ladbroke Grove
This delightful Portuguese patisserie, with
its excellent cakes (including delectable
pasteis de nata custard tarts), is usually full of
regulars sampling coffee and pastries.

SPANISH & PORTUGUESE LONDON

MISCELLANEOUS

BELGIAN

Belgo Noord
72 Chalk Farm Road, NW1
(020-7-267 0718)
Tube: Chalk Farm
Mussels and frites washed down with flavourful Belgian beers are the house speciality at this popular restaurant, with its minimalist décor, robed waiters and bustling atmosphere.

BRAZILIAN

Sabor do Brasil
36 Highgate Hill, N19
(020-7-263 9066)
Tube: Archway
Adding a touch of tropical colour to North London, this brightly-painted, relaxed restaurant serves decent Brazilian food, including classic feijoada, at reasonable prices.

COLOMBIAN

La Tienda
81 Praed Street, W2
(020-7-706 4695)
Open: Mon-Sat 10am-6pm
Tube: Edgware Road or Paddington
This small, laid-back corner store comes complete with a sign which reads 'Parking for Colombians only. All others will be towed'. Beers, spirits and flour are on display, with chorizos and other meats stored in the fridge.

HUNGARIAN

The Gay Hussar
2 Greek Street, W1
(020-7-437 0973)
Tube: Leicester Square or Tottenham Court Road
A venerable Soho restaurant, noted for its literary and political clientele as well as its generous portions of authentic Hungarian food, such as chilled cherry soup and Transylvanian stuffed cabbage.

Louis Patisserie £
32 Heath Street, NW3
(020-7-435 9908)
Tube: Hampstead
Open: Mon-Sun 9.30am-6pm
Set up by Mr Louis over 30 years ago, this charmingly old-fashioned patisserie sells Hungarian cakes and pastries such as dobos (caramel cake) and makos (poppyseed slice), all of which can be enjoyed with a cup of coffee in the tearoom.

The Old Europeans £££
106 High Road, N2
(020-8-883 3964)
Tube: East Finchley
Wooden panelling, folklorie bric-a-brac and violin music add to the atmosphere of this cosy little restaurant, which serves up generous portions of tasty Hungarian dishes, such as paprika pork with tiny dumplings. Chesntnut purée, whipped cream and cherries feature strongly on the dessert list.

MAURITIAN

Chez Liline
101 Stroud Green Road, N4
(020-7-263 6550)
Tube: Finsbury Park
Laid-back and unpretentious, this is a place
to enjoy large portions of delicious
Mauritian seafood, combining both tropical
and French flavours.

MEXICAN

Cool Chile Company
P.O. Box 5702
London W11 2GS
(0870-902 1145)
Also at Portobello Market, on a stall on
Portobello Road, near the junction with Blenheim
Crescent on Saturdays 10.30am-5.30pm.
A must for true connoisseurs of chiles.
Dodie's mail order company offers an
extensive range of dried Central American
chiles from mild guajillo to intensely hot
habaneros, plus Mexican ingredients such as
blue Masa Harina. Dodie is a genuine chile
enthusiast and happy to offer advice and
recipes. For a taste of real Mexican street
food (rather than the Tex-Mex stuff
normally on offer) visit Dodie's stall at
Portobello and enjoy her black bean chile,
quesadilla and guacamole.

SWEDEN

Anna's Place
90 Mildmay Park, N1
(020-7-249 9379)
BR: Canonbury
If you like intimate, homely surroundings
then this pretty restaurant is for you.
Gravadlax, smoked reindeer and Swedish
waffles are among the classic dishes on offer.

Ikea
2 Drury Way
North Circular Road, NW10
(020-8-451 5611)
Open: Mon-Fri 10am-8pm;
Sat 9am-6pm; Sun 11am-5pm
Situated next to the North Circular, this
popular Swedish furniture store has a small
food outlet on the ground floor selling
essentials such as huge circular crispbreads,
gravadlax, lingonberries and frozen Swedish
meatballs.

A Swedish Affair
32 Crawford Street, W1
(020-7-224 9300)
Tube: Baker Street
Open: Mon-Fri 10am-6pm; Sat 10am-5pm
Patriotically painted in yellow and blue (the
colours of the Swedish flag) this pretty shop
has a whole range of Swedish edibles, from
all-important crispbreads and pickled
herrings to treats including liquorice sweets,
lingonberry conserve and Swedish ice
cream. The hard stuff – such as akvavit (an
aromatic spirit) and snuff – is kept behind
the counter.

MISCELLANEOUS

141

KITCHENSHOPS

CENTRAL

The Conran Shop

Michelin House
81 Fulham Road, SW3
(020-7-589 7401)
Tube: South Kensington
Open: Mon & Wed-Sat 9.30am-6pm;
Tue 10am-6pm; Sun 12noon-5pm
This stylish store has a seductive kitchen and
tableware section. Stock ranges from wacky
glass tumblers to exclusive Quaglino china,
and wooden-handled tin openers to elegant
espresso-makers.

Divertimenti

45-47 Wigmore Street, W1
(020-7-935 0689)
Tube: Bond Stret
Open: Mon-Fri 9.30am-6pm;
Sat 10am-5pm
An attractive kitchenware shop which offers
a seductive mixture of colourful ceramic
tableware and cooking utensils. Items range
from nutmeg mills to French steel pans.
They also offer a mail order service.
Also at: *139–141 Fulham Road, SW3*
(020-7–581 8065).

Habitat

196 Tottenham Court Road, W1
(020-7-631 3880)
Tube: Goodge Street
Open: Mon-Wed 10am-6pm;
Thur 10am-8pm; Fri & Sat 10am-6.30pm;
Sun 12 noon-6pm
Piles of saucepans, plates and mugs lend a
bazaar-like quality to the kitchen section
here. Useful for colourful, reasonably-priced
tableware, Habitat also stocks basic pots and
pans. There is an Eastern element too with a
selection of bamboo steamers, woks and
Japanese bowls.

Heal's

196 Tottenham Court Road, W1
Tube: Goodge Street
Open: Mon-Wed 10am-6pm;
Thur 10am-8pm; Fri 10am-6.30pm;
Sat 9.30am-6.30pm
The elegant kitchen section is strong on
stylish gastro-items such as stainless steel
Dualit toasters and Waring blenders. It also
has a select range of cookware and a good
choice of attractive tableware.

Jerry's Home Store

163-167 Fulham Road, SW3
(020-7-581 0909)
Tube: South Kensington
Open: Mon-Sat 10am-6pm;
Sun 12 noon-6pm
Bright and airy, this all–American store has a
good range of upmarket cookware, cheerful
tableware, American cookbooks and kitchen
utensils and gadgets including Waring
blenders, pasta racks and popcorn makers.

John Lewis

Oxford Street, W1
(020-7-629 7711)
Tube: Oxford Circus
Open: Mon-Wed & Fri 9.30am-6pm;
Thur 10am-8pm; Sat 9am-6pm
This large, neatly-arranged kitchenware
department has an excellent range of
cookware, including Circulon, Prestige and
Le Creuset. It also stocks microwave ware,
assorted storage jars, knives and baking
paraphenalia, as well as gadgets including
strawberry hullers, lemon wedge covers and
garni bags. Prices are competitive and staff
are helpful.

Leon Jaeggi
77 Shaftesbury Avenue, W1
(020-7-580 1974/434 4545)
Tube: Leicester Square or Piccadilly Circus
Open: Mon-Sat 9am-5.30pm
A large, well-established shop frequented by
chefs which specialises in professional
catering utensils and equipment including
tin-lined copperware and a huge range of
knives. Stock is extensive and the staff are
helpful and knowledgeable. Note that prices
do not include VAT.

David Mellor
4 Sloane Square, SW1
(020-7-730 4259)
Tube: Sloane Square
Open: Mon-Sat 9.30am-6pm
Classically tasteful stock, including a good
selection of wooden salad bowls and
Mellor's well-designed cutlery.

Pages
121 Shaftesbury Avenue, W1
(020-7-379 6334)
Tube: Leicester Square or
Tottenham Court Road
Open: Mon-Fri 9am-6pm; Sat 9am-5pm
Eye-catching displays of huge ice-sculpture
mounds in the window mark this large,
well-stocked shop, aimed primarily at the
catering trade but also stocking useful items
for home cooks.

Staines Catering Equipment
15-19 Brewer Street, W1
(020-7-437 8424)
Tube: Leicester Square or Piccadilly Circus
Open: Mon-Fri 9am-5pm; Sat 9.30am-2pm
As the name suggests, this shop's stock is
aimed at the catering trade.

NORTH

Richard Dare
93 Regent's Park Road, NW1
(020-7-722 9428)
Tube: Chalk Farm
Open: Mon-Fri 9.30am-6pm;
Sat 10am-4pm
An attractive kitchenware shop, very much
at home in an upmarket parade of shops. It
specialises in French ceramic tableware – a
colourful medley of vivid blues, greens and
yellows.

The Scullery
123 Muswell Hill Broadway, N10
(020-8-444 5236)
Bus: 134
Open: Mon-Sat 9.30am-6pm
A neat, cheery shop with a wide range of
tableware including Portmerion china and
hand-painted dishes, plus kitchen utensils
and cookware.

Gill Wing Cookshop
190 Upper Street, N1
(020-7-226 5392)
Tube: Highbury & Islington
Open: Mon-Sat 9.30am-6pm;
Sun 10am-6pm
A friendly kitchen shop with stock ranging
from stainless steel saucepans to decorative
tableware.

SOUTH

Cookshop
89 The Broadway, SW19
(020-8-543 1010)
Tube: Wimbledon
Open: Mon-Fri 9.30am-5.30pm;
Sat 9.30am-6pm
A general cookshop with stock ranging from
baking tins to woks.

MISCELLANEOUS

La Cuisiniere
81-83 Northcote Road, SW11
(020-7-223 4487)
BR: Clapham Junction
Open: Mon-Sat 9.30am-6pm
The thinking behind of this Aladdin's cave
of a shop is that 'life goes on in the kitchen'.
As a result, stock ranges across from kitchen
and tableware to specialist gadgets, with
friendly staff on hand to proffer advice.

Kooks Unlimited
16 Eton Street, TW10
(020-8-940 8448)
Tube: Richmond
Open: Mon-Sat 9.30am-5.30pm
This small, cheerful shop is crammed with
stock from Le Creuset casserole dishes to
kitchen gadgets.

WEST

Kitchen Ideas
70 Westbourne Grove, W2
Open: Mon-Sat 9.30am-6pm
(020-7-229 3388)
A down-to-earth shop with stock aimed at
the catering trade.
Also at:
23 New Broadway, W5
(020-8-566 5620)
Open: Mon-Sat 9.30am-6pm.

The Kitchenware Company
36 Hill Street, TW9
(020-8-948 7785)
Tube: Richmond
Open: Mon-Sat 9.30am-5.30pm
This well-stocked shop offers a mail order
service. Stock ranges from everyday basics
and gadgets to specialist equipment.

John Russell Kitchenware
128 Chiswick High Road, W4
(020-8-994 5790)
Open: Mon-Sat 10am-6pm
A small, well-stocked shop with a good
range of items, from professional cookware
to attractive tableware.

BOOKSHOPS

Books For Cooks
4 Blenheim Crescent, W11
(020-7-221 1992)
Open: Mon-Sat 9.30am-6pm
This tiny shop-cum-café, crammed with
cookbooks from floor to ceiling, is a mecca
for anyone interested in food and cookery.
The stock is extensive, ranging across
cuisines from Asian to Spanish, and usefully
includes American publications and out-of-
print books. Staff are knowledgeable and
helpful and appetising cooking smells waft
out from the small back kitchen, where
recipes from books stocked in the shop are
tested on the café's customers.

The Africa Centre
38 King Street, WC2
Tube: Covent Garden
(020-7-240 6649)
Open: Mon-Fri 11am-5.30pm;
Sat 11am-5pm
This small bookshop stocks some unusual
and hard-to-find African cookbooks.

The Japan Centre
212 Piccadilly, W1
(020-7-434 4218)
Open: Mon-Sat 10am-7.30pm;
Sun 10am-6pm
A good selection of Japanese cookbooks.

MISCELLANEOUS

The books used for my research include all the cookbooks I've recommended in each section of the book; those listed below are additional sources.

Across Seven Seas *Caroline Adams* (Tharp Books, 1987)
The Best of Thai Cooking *Chalie Amatyakul* (Travel Publishing Asia, 1988)
The British Musuem Cookbook *Michelle Berriedale-Johnson* (British Museum Publications, 1987)
Just Like It Was *Harry Blacker* (Vallentine, Mitchell & Co., 1974)
Fruits and Vegetables of the Caribbean *M.J. Bourne, G.W. Lennox, S.A. Seddon* (Macmillan, 1988)
South East Asian Food *Rosemary Brissenden* (Penguin, 1970)
The Club *Stephen Brook* (Constable, 1989)
Polish Cookbook *Zofia Czerny* (Panstowowe Wydawnictwo Ekonomiczne, 1975)
Galing Galing *Nora and Mariles Daza* (Daza, 1974)
The Fine Art of Japanese Cooking *Hideo Dekura* (Bay Books, n.d.)
Inside Soho *Mark Edmonds* (Robert Nicholson, 1988)
The Streets of East London *William Fishman* (Duckworth, 1979)
Staying Power *Peter Fryer* (Pluto Press, 1984)
Jewish Cookbook *Florence Greenberg* (Hamlyn, 1980).
Jane Grigson's Vegetable Book *Jane Grigson* (Penguin, 1980)
Exotic Fruits and Vegetables *Jane Grigson and Charlotte Knox* (Jonathan Cape, 1986)
Singapore Food *Wendy Hutton* (Times Books International, 1989)
Filipino Cooking Here and Abroad *Eleanor Laquian and Irene Sobrevinas* (National Book Store Inc., 1977)
Old Polish Traditions in the Kitchen and at the Table *Maria Lemnis and Henryk Vitry* (Interpress Publishers, n.d.)
East End Story *A.B. Levy* (Vallentine, Mitchell & Co., 1950)
Guide to Ethnic London *Ian McAuley* (Michael Haag, 1987)
The Peopling of London *Nick Merriman* (The Museum of London, 1993)
A Popular Guide to Chinese Vegetables *Karen Philipps and Martha Dahlen* (Frederick Muller, 1983)
Fruits of South–East Asia *Jacqueline M. Piper* (Oxford University Press, 1989)
Living London *George Sims* (Cassell, 1904–1906)
The Best of Singapore Cooking *Mrs Leong Yee Soo* (Times Books International, 1988)
Penang Nonya Cooking *Cecilia Tan* (Times Books International 1983)
Sushi Made Easy *Nobuko Tsuda* (John Weatherhill Inc, 1982)
The London Encyclopedia *Ben Weinreb and Christopher Hibbert* (Papermac, 1987)
Cooking the Polish-Jewish Way *Eugeniusz Wirkowski* (Interpress Publishers, 1988)
Jewish London *Linda Zoff* (Piatkus, 1986)

INDEX

GASTRO-SOHO TOURS

Aimed at anyone interested in food, Jenny Linford's **Gastro-SohoTours** are guided tours around Soho's diverse and fascinating foodshops. The tours start in Chinatown, exploring the rich treasures of exotic fruits and vegetables and unusual ingredients to be found in chinese supermarkets, pauses for coffee then goes on to explore Soho's European foodshops, from venerable Italian delicatessens to aromatic coffee shops. Throughout the tour foodwriter Jenny Linford offers ingredient information and recommendations, plus recipe suggestions.

For details of **Gastro-Soho Tours** ring 020-8-440 0794

Order Form

Bargain Hunters' London
by Andrew Kershman
0-9522914-2-8   £5.99

A comprehensive guide to finding bargains in the capital including the best charity shops, auctions, designer sales and much more. The book contains 11 area maps and 50 photos.

Museums & Galleries of London by Abigail Willis
0-9522914-3-6   £8.99

A guide combining reviews of all the museums and galleries of London with listings of the commercial galleries, archives and details of London's many art degree shows. The guide contains 50 black and white and 16 colour photos.

Gay London
by Graham Parker
0-9522914-6-0   £6.99

A guide to London's gay scene which doesn't just concentrate on gay clubs (although they are reviewed), but takes a broader look at what's on offer for gay Londoners and visitors to the capital.

Taste of London
by Jenny Linford
9522914-7-9   £6.99

A Taste of London contains over 80 cosmopolitan recipes, many of them recommended by Londoners of diverse ethnic origin and using all the ingredients to be found in the Capital.

The Guide to Cookery Courses by Eric Treuille
0-9522914-9-5   £4.99

This is the only detailed guide to the UK's cookery courses and includes a section on cooking holidays abroad as well as cookware shops, cookbook shops and useful reference information for cooks.

The London Market Guide (2nd Edition)
by Andrew Kershman
£5.99

The second edition of The London Market Guide containing all the essential information to explore London's street markets with maps, photos, travel information and consumer tips.

To order any of the above titles send a cheque (including £1 p&p) to:

Metro Publications
PO Box 6336
London N1 6PY
e-mail: metro@dircon.co.uk

Make your cheque payable to **Metro Publications**
(Please allow 14 days for delivery).

To keep up with Metro's current range of titles visit our web site:
www.metropublications.com